SAGES *of* ANCIENT INDIA

Swami B.B. Tirtha Maharaj

MANDALA

SAGES *of*

ANCIENT INDIA

the SACRED TEACHINGS *of* DHRUVA AND PRAHLAD

by

SWAMI B.B. TIRTHA MAHARAJ

MANDALA
PUBLISHING

MANDALA
PUBLISHING

2240-B 4th Street

San Rafael, CA 94901

t. 415.460.6112

f. 415.460.5218

orders. 800.688.2218

ISBN: 1-886069-58-1

Printed in China by

Palace Press International

Table of Contents

SAGES of ANCIENT INDIA
the Sacred Teachings of Dhruva and Prahlad

Srila Bhakti Ballabh Tirtha Maharaj

Srila Bhakti Dayita Madhava Maharaj

SAGES *of* ANCIENT INDIA
THE SACRED TEACHINGS OF DHRUVA AND PRAHLAD

Preface TO THE ENGLISH EDITION

Sages of Ancient India—The Sacred Teachings of Dhruva and Prahlad is the English rendering of two Bengali narrations, which were compiled by His Holiness Śrīla Bhakti Ballabh Tirtha Maharaj in 1971. The stories of Dhruva Maharaj and Prahlad Maharaj originally occur in the greatest of Indian scriptures, *Śrīmad Bhāgavatam*, which elaborates upon the science of full-fledged theism. Therein is recounted how Dhruva and Prahlad devoted themselves to God, how they dealt with difficulties on their spiritual paths and how they finally achieved self-realization by the grace of the Lord.

Especially in these modern days, when many people tend to invent new and, for the most part, watered-down ideas about spirituality, it seems important to publish works that shed light on the teachings of the great saints of the past. If we study these teachings carefully, we will find that they contain universal truths that apply to all times and ages. Such is the case with *Sages of Ancient India.* Although these stories may contain elements that the modern mind would deem mythological, the underlying spiritual message remains a powerful one. As such, this book is more concerned with transcendental truth than with empirical fact.

The prefaces to the first, second and third Bengali editions of this work were written by the renowned Vaiṣṇava saint, His Holiness Śrīla Bhakti Promode Puri Goswami, who disappeared from our mortal vision in 1999. For the sake of readability we have condensed these three separate prefaces into one foreword. For the same reason we have omitted the many beautiful Sanskrit verses that originally occurred in them. Since we are aware that people who are unfamiliar with the spiritual heritage of ancient India may have difficulty in understanding the technical Sanskrit vocabulary, we have explained some key words in the glossary.

We hope this book will prove to be an inspiration for all those who pursue the spiritual path.

–The Publishers

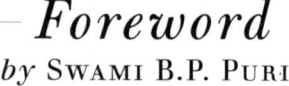

Foreword

by Swami B.P. Puri

The stories of Dhruva Maharaj and Prahlad Maharaj are now appearing in the form of a book due to the unlimited mercy of Śrī Guru, Śrī Gaurāṅga and Śrī Śrī Rādhā-Nayana-Nātha. This is giving us great pleasure. Previously these narrations appeared in the form of articles in several issues of our devotional magazine, *Śrī Chaitanya Vani Patrika*. At the repeated request of many devotees, who wanted to disseminate these stories on a grand scale, it was decided to publish them in the form of a booklet.

When Śrīman Mahāprabhu was residing at Gambhira in Jagannātha Purī after taking *sannyāsa*, He listened innumerable times to the stories of Dhruva and Prahlad from His intimate associate, Śrīla Gadādhara Pandit Goswami. Thus He showed us by His personal example that we should listen very carefully to these narrations again and again. This does not only apply to adults, but to the innocent children as well. We would like these stories to be read to them by their parents, guardians, schoolteachers and well-wishers, because they contain many important teachings regarding the path of devotion.

The holy life of Dhruva exemplifies devotion that was at first tinged with elements of personal desire and then blossomed to complete purity, while the holy life of Prahlad exemplifies devotion that was pure from the onset. Prahlad's worshipable Lord was Śrī Kṛṣṇacandra in the form of Nṛsiṁha *avatāra*, while Dhruva worshiped that same Krishna in the form of the lotus-eyed Lord Śrī Hari, four-armed Vishnu, holding conch-shell, disc, club and lotus. Actually there is no difference in *tattva* (spiritual essence) between the form of Nārāyaṇa (Vishnu) and that of Krishna, yet in the form of Śrī Krishna we find the greater amount of love mellows.

We can observe that, among the nine forms of devotional service, Prahlad was able to attain the Lord by engaging in the process of remembering Him. Dhruva's devotion, however, was mixed with the practice of yoga. Devārṣi Nārada could understand that Dhruva desired to reach a position that had been impossible to attain even by his father and grandfather before him, and he knew that Dhruva's mother had suggested to him that the best way to reach his goal was to worship the Lord by performing yoga. Hence, Dhruva went to Madhuvana, the best among the twelve forests of Vṛndāvana, and purified himself by bathing three times a day in the holy Yamunā River.

On the bank of the Yamunā, Dhruva prepared a suitable sitting place and practiced *prāṇayama* by controlling the inhalation, exhalation and retention of his breath, by fixing his consciousness on Lord Vāsudeva and by meditating upon and visualizing the very powerful and secret twelve-syllable mantra. He also worshiped Lord Vāsudeva with proper *pūjā* articles, all according to the instructions of Nārada Muni. That place in Madhuvana, near Mathura, where Dhruva prepared his *āsana*, is called "Dhruva-tila" ("Dhruva's hill"). Pilgrimages are made there during the first day of Vrajamaṇḍala Parikrama.

Since the Lord is the Supreme Soul and Internal Guru of everyone, He knew the desire of Dhruva's heart and arranged for him to meet a devotee teacher in the form of Nārada Muni. Devārṣi Nārada gave him initiation into the mantra and instructed him on the practice of devotional service. After duly receiving initiation, Dhruva surrendered with great faith to the instructions of his spiritual master and, following a path of firm renunciation, obtained the personal presence of the Lord after having worshiped Him for six months.

Śrī Hari, who is very affectionate to His devotees and eagerly fulfills their desires, knew Dhruva's strong determination and touched the forehead of His devotee with His Panchajanya, the divine conch-shell that bestows pure knowledge. Then Dhruva, in a state of devotional ecstasy, started to compose beautiful verses. Although he was still an illiterate child, these verses are difficult to understand even for great scholars.

The Lord says:

teṣām evānukampārtham
aham ajñāna-jaṁ tamaḥ
nāśayāmy ātma-bhāva-stho
jñāna-dīpena bhāsvatā
(Bhagavad-gītā, 10.11)

Śrīla Bhaktivinoda Ṭhākura explains this verse by saying, "The infinitesimal living entity will never be able to understand or know the Unlimited Absolute Truth by his own endeavor or study, and will never reach the pure knowledge of Truth through many discussions. Only if the Lord blesses the living entity by His inconceivable potency, will the tiny soul be able to directly see and realize that supreme knowledge. Those who are pure devotees of the Lord can easily meditate on Him because the Lord Himself is enlightening them with His transcendental knowledge. The Lord resides in the heart of His devotee and, by His unlimited mercy, completely dispels the darkness of ignorance created by contact with matter. The pure knowledge which can be attained by the soul through devotion will never arise from mere mental exercises based upon speculation and theorizing."

Dhruva's prayers express the gradual detachment from his previous material desires, despite the Lord having agreed to fulfill his wish for opulence by granting him the planet Dhruva-loka, the topmost position above all the three worlds. This planet is in the center of the orbits of the Seven Ṛṣis, the forest hermits and all the stars, including the abodes of the demigods like Dharma, Agni, Kaśyapa and Indra.

Although situated within the material universe, Dhruvaloka is a very unique place—a spiritual planet. It is the residence of Śrī Hari, like Śvetadvīpa, Mathurā, Dvārakā and so on. This planet is not subject to destruction even at the time of the great cosmic annihilation. The Lord gave Dhruva dominion over his father's kingdom for 36,000 years. By worshiping the Lord with the performance of the *dakṣina-bahula yajña*, Dhruva obtained great material pleasures, and at the end of his earthly reign he had the good fortune to reach the supreme destination. The Lord said, "At the end you will be able to reach My supreme abode—My own planet, situated above the abodes of the Ṛṣis, which is considered worshipable by all other planets. Those saints who reach that place will never fall down from there."

The Lord, who is very affectionate to His devotees, granted Dhruva the supreme destination, but He did not give the same blessing to his stepbrother, Uttama, and his stepmother, Suruci, who had committed offenses. Uttama was killed by the Yakṣas while he was hunting in the forest, and Suruci died in a forest fire while searching for him. *Sva-karma phala bhuk puman*: everyone reaps the fruits of his own activities.

The piety and devotion of Sunīti Devī, the mother of Dhruva and the jewel amongst all mothers, is so extraordinary. Although she could well understand the hateful words that her co-wife Suruci had hurled at the little child she had fed at her breast, she told him, "Dear boy, you should not think that your troubles are coming from some other person, because everyone in this life simply gets the same sufferings which he had inflicted upon others in previous lifetimes. If you want to sit on the king's throne like Uttama, you should give up all your hostile thoughts and follow your stepmother's advice, dedicating yourself to the worship of Lord Hari. Her words were true, so you should sincerely do what she said."

Sunīti had given up all hatred and instructed her son to worship the Lord. Dhruva eagerly accepted his mother's words and, with her permission, left to execute her instructions. Such was the extent of Sunīti's surrender to the Lord. What mother would be able to allow her beloved little child, the baby she had carried in her womb, to go to the forest to worship the Lord? This world would be so peaceful if all mothers were to follow the example of this great woman. There would be perfect peace on the face of the Earth. And how much suffering King Uttānapāda bore for having ill-treated his son! Therefore the Lord, who is affectionate to His devotees, also blessed them with the supreme destination.

If someone tastes a little of the nectar of Krishna consciousness, he will naturally forget everything else, just as by eating a small quantity of sweets one's appetite is completely satiated.

We fondly desire that this book will be widely distributed.

If someone tastes a little of the nectar of Krishna consciousness, he will naturally forget everything else, just as by eating a small quantity of sweets one's appetite is completely satiated.

Śrī Vaiṣṇava-dāsa-anudāsa Tridaṇḍi Bhikṣu—
Śrī Bhakti Promode Puri

The Story of Bhakta Dhruva

The Story of Bhakta Dhruva

Once Lord Brahmā was meditating on the manifestation of the universe. As a result, a male and female appeared from him, by the names of Svāyambhuva Manu and Śatarūpā. Svāyambhuva Manu took Śatarūpā as his wife and with her he begot two sons, named Priyavrata and Uttānapāda. These two sons were both empowered by the Supreme Lord, and they appeared for the purpose of protecting the universe.

Uttānapāda became a great king. He had two wives named Sunīti and Suruci. Although Sunīti was the first wife and chief queen, Suruci was the king's favorite. It so happened that Sunīti gave birth to the firstborn son of the king, who was called Dhruva, while Suruci gave birth to a second son, named Uttama.

One day King Uttānapāda took Uttama on his lap, showing him great affection. Seeing this, Dhruva became equally desirous for his father's affection and repeatedly tried to climb on his lap. The king, however, did not have the courage to take Dhruva on his lap in front of Suruci. Knowing of her pride, he was afraid to displease her in any way.

When Suruci saw Dhruva trying to climb on to the lap of his father, she felt a burning hatred inside her heart, and in front of the king she began to insult Dhruva by saying, "Dhruva, my dear boy. You may be the son of the king, but that does not make you worthy to sit on his throne or on his lap. You may not be aware of it, but the king does not like your mother. Surely you

Bhakta Druva in meditation within the forest

are the child of a most unfortunate woman. The king loves me more, and therefore there is no doubt that my son Uttama will sit on his throne. Oh, you pitiable child, there is no hope to fulfill your desire. If you really want to obtain the king's throne, there is only one thing you can do, and I shall tell you the method: pray to the Supreme Lord. When He becomes satisfied by your prayers, the Supreme Lord will come to give you a boon. Then you should ask Him to grant you the blessing to be born again from my womb. Only if you take birth from me, will you be able to sit on the lap of your father. Otherwise, as long as you are the son of such an unfortunate woman, you will never be able to sit on the king's throne in this king's family."

While listening to the piercing words of his stepmother, Dhruva noticed that his father did not even say a single word to stop her. As a result, Dhruva became overwhelmed by a mixture of grief, anger and wounded pride. Crying intensely as though he were a snake beaten with a stick, he ran to his mother. Mother Sunīti saw little Dhruva coming to her with his eyes full of tears, his lips trembling and his lungs heaving heavily. She took the child affectionately on her lap and held him to her bosom in a vain attempt to console him. Dhruva was in such a state that he was completely unable to stop crying or even tell her the reason for his grief. Upon seeing this, Queen Sunīti became very perturbed.

In the meantime, some of the palace maidservants came to Sunīti's courtyard to relate what had actually happened, as they had witnessed the events with their own eyes. After they had finished telling their story, Sunīti could understand why her son was so bereaved, and she hugged him, although she herself was struck with grief. The more she thought about the harsh words of her co-wife Suruci, the more her beautiful lotus eyes poured incessant tears.

After lamenting and weeping for a long time, she tried to regain her composure. She realized that no one would come to give them solace and that there was no way to end their sorrow. She resolved that, for the sake of her son, she should not become distraught but instead should try to give solace to him. Restraining her emotions with great effort, she explained to Dhruva, "My little Dhruva, why are you crying? Why do you suffer so much? Please do not think that your stepmother has caused your suffering. This is not her fault. You must understand that all living beings suffer according to their past activities. Whatever suffering you have inflicted upon others, you will have to accept yourself. The Supreme Lord is the controller of everyone and He awards everyone the results of their past activities. Your suffering is due only to your own *karma*. Your stepmother is not responsible for this and she is not to be blamed; she is only acting as an instrument of the Supreme Lord. Do not be angry with her. I am so unfortunate, and you are equally unfortunate. But, when you think about your misfortune, you should not feel any great pain. My dear Dhruva, we need not grieve over our situation. Although your stepmother has spoken harshly to you, her words are true. Otherwise, how can it be that, in spite of my being the chief queen, the king has come to neglect me like this after accepting me as a wife?"

"Even if the son of a maidservant approaches the king," Sunīti continued, "he will welcome him, caress him with affection and talk with him; but you were not treated like that. The king could have said a few words to console you, but he did not. My dear Dhruva, don't cry any more over this, because by crying we will not obtain any good result. Your stepmother told you to pray to Lord Hari. That was very good advice indeed and I can only offer you the same suggestion. Worship Śrī Hari, leaving aside your anger and ill feelings toward your stepmother, who is not responsible for all this. I have strong faith that you will, one day, come to sit on the king's throne, just like your brother Uttama. The inconceivable Lord Śrī Adhokṣaja, who cannot be known through the material senses, protects the entire universe. Even the great yogis, who have completely controlled their minds and senses, meditate solely on the lotus feet of Śrī Hari. By serving Śrī Hari, your forefather Lord Brahmā obtained the shelter of His lotus feet, which is the best position possible. Also your grandfather, Svāyambhuva Manu, performed the *dakṣiṇa-bahula* sacrifice with great concentration only for the pleasure of Śrī Hari, and he was awarded a very exalted position in this life and in the next, which is very difficult for others to obtain. Therefore, my beloved Dhruva, those who desire liberation try to get the shelter of the lotus feet of Śrī Hari and worship Him to attain their goal. So, you should purify your heart and consciousness with strong determination and, by serving His lotus feet, call for Śrī Hari to come and be seated within your heart. My dear boy, only the lotus-eyed Śrī Hari can solve your problem and no one else. Even Brahmā and the other demigods offer their humble obeisances to and meditate on Lakṣmī Devī, the goddess of fortune, while this same effulgent Lakṣmī is eagerly desiring to serve Śrī Hari with all opulence."

After listening to his mother's lamentation and instruction, Dhruva stopped crying and regained his intelligence, self-control and patience. He began to think, "From what I have heard, if Śrī Hari will be pleased, then I may acquire a kingdom greater than that of my father, or even greater than that of my grandfather, Manu, or that of my forefather, Brahmā, who is the controller of the whole universe." As of that moment, he became resolutely determined to please Śrī Hari. Prince Dhruva was only five years old when he left his father's house and went to the forest to search out Śrī Hari with undivided attention.

Shortly after this incident, Devārṣi Nārada, the divine messenger of the Lord, came to visit the kingdom of King Uttānapāda. He heard from the citizens that Dhruva, the first-born son of the king, had been insulted by his stepmother and, unable to tolerate her harsh words, had left his house and family and had gone to the forest to worship the Lord. Nārada was very astonished to hear that such a small child, only five years old, accustomed to a comfortable life in the palace and pampered by everyone, had taken up such a difficult life of austerity without any prior training.

While Śrī Nārada was thinking in this way, Dhruva was wandering around the forest without food or sleep, calling out continuously, "Where is my lotus-eyed Lord? Where is my lotus-eyed Lord?" Suddenly, Nārada Muni appeared before him and blessed him with great affection. By touching Dhruva's head with his hand, Nārada removed all inauspiciousness. Nārada, upon seeing the boy, said to himself, "How amazing are the pride and intolerance of the *kṣatriya* [warrior] class! Although Dhruva is only a small boy, still now the harsh words of his stepmother are tormenting his heart."

Nārada spoke to Dhruva, "My dear son, you are only a five-year-old child. At this age, children are supposed to be engaged in play. I cannot understand why you are taking all this so seriously. It is only natural that children are sometimes shown affection and sometimes scolded. If, at such a young age, you can discriminate between respect and abuse, then you should also not become confused or dissatisfied, because in this world each and every soul is getting happiness, distress, respect and abuse according to his own *karma*, and not because of someone else's responsibility. No one can get the results of his actions without the consent of the Lord. When you realize this, you will be able to understand that whatever happens in this life is a result of the activities of your past life. Therefore, intelligent persons should never be dissatisfied with what they receive. Since all results of *karma* are under the control of the Lord, whether it be happiness or distress, it would be better for you to go back home and be content by staying there."

After a short pause, Nārada continued, "If, however, you still have the desire to follow your mother's instructions to worship Lord Hari to get His mercy, you should know that worship of the Supreme Lord is not something easy and accessible to all. Even the great *munis* must leave everything behind and renounce attachment to material things. With great determination and potency, they engage in the practice of yoga to reach *samādhi*. Striving for many lifetimes to attain success, they are still not able to know the Supreme Lord. Given this, how could a small child like you try to obtain the fruits of this worship within a short time? You should abandon this idea. Childhood or boyhood is not the proper time to engage in *hari-bhajana* [exclusive worship of the Lord] as the best time for the observance of religious duties is old age. I advise you to take an interest in transcendental topics when you become old, not now. If you can understand your happiness and distress to be the will or mercy of the Supreme Lord, then you will have no reason to feel dissatisfied. Every person is receiving the good and bad fruits of their *karma*. By simply meditating on Śrī Hari, one can find satisfaction and obtain liberation from the cycle of birth and death. If one sees someone more qualified than himself, he should develop affection for such a person and try to serve him; if one sees someone less qualified, he should show mercy toward him, and, if one sees someone equally qualified, he should make friends with him. In this way, one will never feel disappointed or sorrowful."

After listening to the instructions of Nārada Muni, Dhruva only became more and more determined in his plan and said, "In happiness or distress a person's mind can become confused. Your nature is such that, due to your mercy, you approach these confused persons to instruct them on how to find the way to peace. But, for me, this is very difficult to accept. I am impatient because that is the nature of the *kṣatriyas*—that is why my nature is that of intolerance. The arrows of the hard words of Suruci have pierced my heart. Therefore, your instructions cannot find a resting place in this pierced heart of mine. O *brāhmaṇa*! The supreme position in the three worlds, which could not be attained by my father or all my forefathers, is the position to which I wish to ascend. So please tell me an easy way to achieve this. You are so glorious—you have appeared from the very body of Lord Brahmā. You always sanctify the universe by moving here and there like the sun, while chanting the glories of Śrī Hari and playing on your vina."

Nārada, the best of devotees, was very pleased to hear Dhruva speak like this and to see his firm resolve in wishing to worship Śrī Hari. At first, he wanted to test Dhruva's faith and therefore he tried to discourage him from worshiping the Lord. But Dhruva replied, "If I do not attain the lotus feet of Śrī Hari, I will never return home again." Seeing such strong faith, Nārada was pleased in his heart and blessed the young boy with his causeless mercy. He then gave him some instructions on an easy way to perform the worship of Śrī Hari.

Nārada said, "My dear Dhruva, up till now I have said so many things just to test your faith, but I am very satisfied to see your strong determination. You should understand that the instructions your mother Sunīti has given you are the best instructions possible. The practice of love and devotion to Śrī Hari is the topmost and most auspicious practice, and the only easy way to obtain the Lord's lotus feet. For the Lord it is possible to fulfill all the desires of the living entity. If someone desires to obtain *artha, kāma, dharma* or *mokṣa*, the only way to reach his goal is to serve the lotus feet of Śrī Vishnu with full dedication. Therefore, my dear Dhruva, I am blessing you: may you obtain all success. Go to the bank of the River Yamunā, to the forest of Madhuvana—a place that is very dear to Śrī Hari. There you should bathe regularly three times a day in the pure waters of Kalindi, and after performing your duties you should sit down and practice *prāṇayama* by inhaling and exhaling your breath with full control. After quieting the restless mind and senses, make your consciousness steady and meditate on Śrī Vāsudeva, the guru of the entire world."

Dhruva had completely surrendered himself unto the lotus feet of his guru, so he made a vow to execute his orders. Nārada gave him a special mantra and specific instructions on how to properly meditate on Śrī Hari, saying, "Here is how you are to meditate on the form of Śrī Hari. Śrī Hari's body and countenance radiate contentment, satisfaction and the desire to bestow mercy. His nose is beautiful, His eyebrows are very attractive and also His neck is splendid. His person is the most wonderful. He is eternally young, His limbs are extremely attractive, and His lips and eyes have the hue of the rising sun. He is the only shelter for everyone, the supreme form of all that is to be achieved and He is an ocean of mercy. His eyes are full of love and the right side of His chest bears the mark of Śrīvatsa. His complexion is darkish like a new monsoon cloud, He wears a garland made of forest flowers and His four arms hold the conch-shell, disc, club and lotus. He is decorated by a crown, two beautiful earrings, bracelets and bangles. On His neck rests the Kauṣṭubha Jewel. His exquisite upper and lower garments are yellow, and He wears a waist belt and brilliant anklets at His feet. His form is the most beautiful thing one could ever see and increases the pleasure of the eyes of His pure devotees who long to serve Him. His beautiful feet, with nails shining like pearls, are resting on the lotus hearts of those who have the power of devotion. His sweet smile and affectionate looks are always bestowing mercy upon His devotees. Dear Dhruva, you should meditate on Śrī Hari, the greatest of all those who can give boons, with fully controlled mind and concentrated consciousness, as I have just told you. If you constantly meditate on the all-auspicious Lord, you will rapidly achieve a peace of mind you will never lose."

Nārada continued, "O son of the king, I am now teaching you the most secret mantra: '*oṁ namo bhagavate vāsudevāya.*' If you chant this mantra sincerely for seven nights, you will be able to see the associates of the Lord moving in the sky. Those learned persons, who know the proper place and time, worship Lord Vāsudeva with this mantra and a full variety of *pūjā* articles. You are to perform the worship of Vāsudeva by, first of all, preparing the necessary paraphernalia: sanctified water, garlands, fruits and roots collected in the forest, nice *darbha* grass tips, garments made of soft leaves, bark from the plantain tree, and *tulasī* , which is very dear to the Lord. Try to make nice arrangements for the worship of the Deity of the Lord. If nothing else is available, you may even worship Lord Nārāyaṇa with only soil and water. When someone worships the Lord, he should do so with fixed consciousness, in a peaceful and mind-

Narada Muni teaching Dhruva the process of meditation

ful state, controlling his speech, eating moderately and avoiding foods not having the quality of goodness. The Lord has many inconceivable forms and potencies, by which He appears by His own sweet will, in different *avatāras* and *līlās*. You should meditate on the Lord, who is described by the most beautiful of prayers. You should likewise meditate on His *avatāras* and His inimitable character. If a person offers to the Lord a variety of articles such as perfume, sandal paste, betel nut, umbrella, fan etc., following the method shown by the great devotees of the past, then that worship should also be accompanied by the twelve-syllable mantra, a sound representation of the Lord. If someone humbly executes this method of worship with body, mind and words, offering his service with love and devotion, the Lord will always bless him with the fulfillment of all his desires—*artha, kāma, dharma* or *mokṣa*. But if that person is a surrendered soul who has taken shelter of the lotus feet of a pure devotee, then, for his service, the Lord will give him much more than what he desires: He will grant him *prema-bhakti*. That person, who has already tasted (and therefore is already fully satiated by) *artha, kāma* and *dharma*, who is not attracted by *mokṣa,* and who sees no particular value in *jñāna* or *karma,* will pursue with great determination the path of *bhakti- yoga* to obtain *prema-bhakti* itself through his worship of the Lord."

After Nārada had taught him the authorized system for worshiping Śrī Hari, Dhruva offered his obeisances to the lotus feet of his guru and circumambulated him. He then went to the forest of Madhuvana (which is decorated by the marks of the Lord's feet), where he would perform his austerity.

Meanwhile, Nārada went to the palace of King Uttānapāda and entered his apartments. The king welcomed the Devārṣi by offering him all appropriate paraphernalia and a seat. After that, he offered Nārada scented water and washed his feet. Nārada sat down comfortably and spoke as follows: "O king, I see from your forlorn expression that something has been troubling you for some time. What is the matter? Are you experiencing any problems with the pursuance of your *artha, kāma* or *dharma*? Does someone of your kith and kin suffer from any problem? Has anything dangerous or harmful happened?"

The king answered in a voice filled with sadness, "O Nārada, I am worried about my little child, a five-year-old boy, who is very intelligent. Oh, shame on me! I have been so cruel to send away this boy and his mother because of my attachment to a woman. O lord, that good-natured boy is now without shelter. Who will look after him and protect him? How much pain he must be feeling, walking on the forest paths which are so full of thorns! Who will provide food for him in the forest? O Devārṣi, I cannot find peace, thinking of the sad face of my hungry child. Do tell me, is he still alive, or has he been devoured by a tiger or another ferocious animal, unable as he is to protect himself? Just see how hard-hearted I have been! This child wanted to climb on my lap, motivated by his affection, but I did not even grant him a sweet word. I behaved like the lowest of men, because of attachment to my wife! O Devārṣi, my heart has become very restless thinking about my innocent son Dhruva."

Upon hearing the tragic plight of the king, Nārada said, "Dear king, why are you lamenting for your son? No misfortune has befallen him, because he is protected by the *devas*. Very soon you will witness his return. Your son's fame will be spread all over the universe. You are unaware of his glories and thus your sorrow is meaningless. O king, whatever opulence could not be attained by any king of the past, your Dhruva will obtain by worshiping the Lord. After achieving this, he will come back." While listening to Nārada's description of the glories of his son, King Uttānapāda became absorbed in thinking of Dhruva and soon forgot his undue attachment to the queen.

Meanwhile, Dhruva was performing his austere *sādhana*. He bathed in the water of the Yamunā and fasted all night. According to the instructions of Nārada, he concentrated upon controlling his senses and began to worship Śrī Hari, the Supreme Person. He began practicing a very intense austerity. In the first month he ate a small amount of *bel* or *badari* fruits every three days, just enough for his bare survival. In the second month he stopped eating fruits and instead, every six days, took only dry leaves that had fallen from trees, and started his service to the Lord from that point. In the third month, he began to take only water every nine days, while still meditating on the Lord with full consciousness.

In the fourth month, for sustenance, he was only breathing air once every twelve days and, in this way, he conquered his breathing power, all the while meditating on Śrī Nārāyaṇa. In the fifth month, after conquering his *prāṇa*, Prince Dhruva stood still on one leg without moving, like a stick, and meditated on the Supreme with undivided attention. He silenced his mind and stopped all the activities of his knowledge-acquiring senses (eyes, ears, nose, tongue and skin) and their related objects of perception (form, sound, smell, taste and touch). In his heart, he gave up the desire for any object of attraction except the desire to behold the form of the Lord. Thus, he entered *samādhi*.

In this sublime trancelike state, Dhruva could not see anything except the form of the Lord. He was standing on his toes and the earth became so disturbed by his austerity that it started to shake and almost fell from its orbit. The violence of this motion was just like a small boat, rocking from one side to the other due to the movements of an elephant attempting to step into it. When Dhruva closed the doors of his *prāṇa* and started to meditate on Śrī Vishnu, the Soul of the universe, all the *devas* and the inhabitants of their planets started choking and felt intolerable suffering because of their inability to breathe. The *devas* could not understand the reason for their suffering. They decided to take shelter of Śrī Hari and started praying to Him to free them from their pain, saying, "O Lord, all the movable and immovable living entities are now breathless. We have never experienced anything like this before. You are our only Shelter and Protector. We take shelter of You, please save us from this suffocation."

The Lord, moved by their earnest supplications, said, "O *devas*, this choking is caused by a child in Madhuvana Forest. I shall stop his *tapasya*. Dhruva, the son of Uttānapāda, has become so absorbed in his meditation upon Me that he cannot think of anything else. You should have no fear in this regard. Please go back to your respective abodes." Indra and all the other *devas* were reassured by the words of Śrī Hari, and, after offering Him obeisances, they returned to their heavenly realm. Desirous of seeing His own devotee, the Lord mounted His divine carrier, Garuḍa, and flew to Madhuvana Forest.

Dhruva was meditating on the Lord's form with one-pointed attention and closed eyes. In his spiritual trance, he suddenly felt a flash in his lotus heart, as if Śrī Hari had personally appeared. He opened his eyes and the exact form that he had been contemplating in his mind now appeared before his eyes. After seeing the Lord, Dhruva offered Him his respectful obeisances by falling flat onto the ground like a stick. The inconceivable, beautiful form of the Lord fascinated him. His mind was firmly fixed upon the Lord and his eyes thirstily drank the sweetness of His form. He kissed Him with his mouth and embraced Him with his arms.

Śrī Hari is none other than the Supreme Soul, residing in the heart of all living entities. Since He knows the hearts of everyone, He could understand Dhruva's feelings. Five-year-old Dhruva stood with folded hands and, out of feelings of intense longing, fervently desired to offer prayers of glorification to the Lord but, due to his immaturity, he was unable to express his feelings adequately in words. The merciful Lord could understand this and, out of compassion for him, He touched the throat of Dhruva with His conch-shell, Pāñcajañya, which has the capacity to bestow divine knowledge. The touch of that divine conch-shell conferred upon Dhruva great power of speech. Expressions of the utmost eloquence and refinement danced on his tongue—deep realizations of the truth of soul and Supersoul. All of this came to him in the most natural way. Dhruva's heart drowned in devotion, while his mind basked in the greatness of the glory of the Lord. He started to pray:

"Oh Lord and Master of all potencies! By Your own *cit-śakti*, You have entered my mind and given life to hitherto hidden powers of articulation and to all my senses. I offer my obeisances unto You, O Supreme Person, knower of everything. Only by Your *māyā* is this endless universe created and You have entered into it in the form of Paramātmā, just like fire, that is one in essence, appears in many different kinds of firewood. Similarly, You manifest Yourself in many different ways, giving shelter to the senses of the liberated and conditioned souls alike. O Friend of those afflicted by miseries! Just as a person who wakes up from sleep is able to see everything in the universe and perceive that he is indeed seeing, similarly Lord Brahmā, by completely surrendering to Your feet, became aware of the real form of the universe and, simultaneously, became aware of his own ability to perceive. O Lord! Your lotus feet are the only refuge of the liberated souls, because all those who have taken shelter of them have reached actual liberation. Therefore, how can they ever forget You, when they have been helped so much by You? You fulfill all the desires of the living entities, even the desires of those who are already liberated from the cycle of birth and death, because You give them something immeasurably more valuable—Your eternal service. Therefore, if those who, by Your causeless mercy, obtain Your unconditional eternal service desire something other than Your loving service, they are actually foolish and cheated by *māyā*, because they want sense gratification for this body, which consists of dull and inert matter. All these objects of sense pleasure are always obtainable even for the residents of hell. O Lord, meditating on Your lotus feet and listening to the descriptions of Your character in the company of Your devotees provides a pleasure which cannot be compared to the *brahmānanda* or heavenly pleasures, what to speak of the lower material pleasures, because time is knocking the *devas* from heaven and throwing them down into this world. O Ananta, those who are pure souls are always Your devotees. Please grant me the proper company of those great souls because, if I listen to Your nectarean pastimes in the association of such pure devotees, I will be able to taste a deep and constant bliss of sublime purity, while escaping the greatest sufferings of this ocean of birth and death. O Padmanabha, those whose hearts' desire is to enjoy the scent of Your lotus feet look for the proper association of the great souls; they do not develop an excessive attachment for this body and for what is related to it—wife, children, friends, house, riches, etc. They do not dwell upon all these material things. O Lord of lords, I know all the invisible and visible things included in Your Universal Form, such as the *mahat-tattva* and the five gross elements, the human beings, *devas*, demons, reptiles, mountains, trees, birds and animals, but I do not know anything of Your spiritual form. At the time of dissolution, this *Purūṣa* winds up all the universes within His abdomen and lies down in mystic slumber on the serpentine bedstead of Ananta Śeṣa. From His navel sprouts a brilliant golden lotus. I offer my obeisances to that *Purūṣa*. O Lord, You are eternally liberated, unlike the *jīvā* who is able to get liberation only by dint of Your mercy. You are supremely pure, while the individual soul is impure. You know everything, while the *jīvā* knows very little. You are the Lord of illusion, while the *jīvā* dwells in the clutches of illusion. You are immutable, while the *jīvā* constantly undergoes change by coming into contact with the fickle finger of *māyā*. You are the Original Person, and the *jīvā* is born from You. You are full of all opulence, while the *jīvā* has very little opulence. You control the three *guṇas*, while the *jīvā's* quality is to be attracted by them. You always see everything and every position by means of Your *cit-śakti* and therefore you are totally different from the *jīvās*, who are in constant opposition to each other due to the bewildering influence of the *guṇas*. All unlimited potencies emanate from God, Who is the form of all inconceivable potencies, the eternal origin of the universe, without origin, limitless, full of bliss, immutable, the Supreme Brahman. I have surrendered unto the lotus feet of this Lord. O Lord, those who know that You are the only *puruṣārtha*—the most valuable asset to pursue in one's life—worship You as the form of supreme bliss. For them, Your lotus feet are more valuable than any kingdom. A cow is full of affection for her newborn calf, giving him milk to drink and protecting him from ferocious animals. Similarly, by dint of Your great potency, You are inclined to

bless with affection those who, like me, worship You with some ulterior motive, protecting them from the fearful ocean of birth and death."

Dhruva's invocations greatly pleased the Lord, Who is always affectionate to His devotees. Desiring to grant him a boon, the Lord spoke thus: "O prince, you have fulfilled your vows perfectly. I am blessing you with all good fortune. I know what you desire and I shall award you a most brilliant position in a place difficult to achieve. This rare place will never be destroyed. Its name will be Dhruvaloka. Until now, no one has been able to attain that place, which is always near the planets, the stars and the constellations. The planets of the great powerful sages will last until the end of the *kalpa* [a time of great cosmic dissolution], but your planet will never perish. That planet is always near to the abodes of Dharma, Agni, Kaśyapa, Indra, the Seven Ṛṣis, the forest hermits and the other stars. These abodes of the *devas* and the sages always revolve around your planet [in Vedic cosmology, all celestial objects orbit relative to a fixed point, the pole star—Dhruvaloka]. Dear boy, very soon your father will hand over his kingdom to you and will retire to the forest. With steadfast intelligence and adherence to the principles of *dharma,* you will protect this earthly kingdom for 36,000 years. Your brother Uttama will be lost in the forest while hunting. His mother Suruci will leave the palace to search for him, and will become trapped in a forest fire. I am the personification of yoga. Therefore, you will worship Me through yoga practice and present Me suitable offerings according to your position. This will enable you to obtain the greatest pleasures in the world. At the end of your life you will be able to remember Me and reach My abode, the supreme planet worshiped by all planets, which is beyond the abode of the Ṛṣis. Those who renounce the material world will never fall down from that place, once they have reached it." After giving this boon and these instructions to little Dhruva, Śrī Hari left with Garuḍa to His own abode. Thus, Dhruva obtained service to the lotus feet of Śrī Hari, the most rare of gifts. The lotus feet of the Lord alleviate the tendency of the mind to search futilely for happiness divorced from the very source of happiness, Śrī Krishna.

Still, Dhruva was not yet fully satisfied. According to the order he had received from Śrī Hari, he departed for his father's house. While on his return journey, Dhruva remembered the harsh and intolerable words of his stepmother, which had pierced his heart to the core. Realizing that he had not thought to ask the Lord for the most precious of all boons, unalloyed devotional service to Him, he reproached himself bitterly. "Ah, how unhappy I am! Alas! The great *munis,* who strictly observe vows of celibacy, reach their position only after many lifetimes of great *tapasya.*

I, on the other hand, obtained the shelter of the lotus feet of the Lord after only six months and, even then, with distracted vision. And now I have again fallen into *saṁsāra* from that position. Alas! What ill fate! What misfortune! Just see how foolish I am! Although I obtained the lotus feet of Śrī Hari, which destroy all material conditioning, I prayed for a temporary kingdom. I think that this mishap was caused by the *devas*, who became envious as they could not tolerate the fact that I received a kingdom higher than theirs. Otherwise, how could I possibly have rejected the instructions that Devārṣi Nārada had given me intended for my own benefit? There is no one more unfortunate than I! Like a person feeling great fear and pain while dreaming of a wild animal attacking him, I have been confused by *māyā* into dualistic thinking and was unable to desire the Lord only. Rather, I have been thinking of my brother as my enemy. This thought is causing me great pain. It is very difficult to please Śrī Hari, the Soul of the universe, by one's own *tapasya*. But see: I succeeded in pleasing Him, yet I prayed to Him for temporary things. I prayed for things that are useless, just as medicines are useless to a person who is about to die. As a poor man approaches a great emperor, the sovereign of the whole world, to beg for a few grains of broken rice with its husk, similarly, in my misfortune, I prayed to Śrī Hari to get some small things of insignificant value. Śrī Hari wanted to give me the service of His lotus feet, but due to my foolishness I prayed for something to satisfy my pride. Ah, fie on me, one hundred times!"

While his son Dhruva was on his way back home, King Uttānapāda was informed about his return. At first, he could not believe it. Who would take seriously the news of the return of someone who had died? The King thought to himself, "How can I believe that Dhruva is returning home again? What pious deeds have I performed in order to get him back? From where is this good fortune coming?" Then the king remembered the words of Devārṣi Nārada, who had foretold that his child would come back soon. The idea of seeing his son again almost drove the king mad with happiness and, reflecting again upon what he had done to Dhruva, he began to reproach himself. Then, in an ebullient mood, he presented the messenger of good tidings with a very valuable gold chain.

Maharaj Uttānapāda felt so excited about the return of his son that he was feeling restless and could not remain in his house. He gave orders to prepare a chariot, decorated with gold and pulled by beautiful, swift horses. The king hastened out of the palace and ascended the chariot. Amidst the sound of conchshells, trumpets, flutes, and the loud chanting of Vedic hymns, he departed to meet his son, accompanied by *brāhmaṇas*, dignitaries, ministers and all of his friends.

After a short time, the party arrived at the edge of the forest and they could see Dhruva approaching. Having been bereft of the company of his son and thinking him to have died, the king was so excited and anxious to see him that he was laboring heavily with uninhibited emotion. Descending from his chariot, he quickly approached the boy and embraced him tightly with both arms. Dhruva, however, did not feel strongly attached to him, because the touch of the lotus feet of Śrī Nārāyaṇa had cut asunder the knots of material bondage. Uttānapāda was kissing his son's head again and again, drenching his body with tears of joy.

Dhruva, the best of good-hearted persons, first offered obeisances to his father's feet. His father blessed him with full affection and greeted him by saying, "Dear Dhruva, are you well?" After that, Dhruva offered his respects to his two mothers, Sunīti and Suruci, by prostrating himself. Seeing the child prostrated at her feet, Suruci embraced him affectionately and made him get up. With a faint and half-choked voice she blessed him, saying, "Dear boy, may you live long! Those who have been blessed with friendship, affection, mercy and love by Śrī Hari, having pleased Him with their good qualities, will always be respected and loved by all souls, just as water always runs downward."

Then, Dhruva met Uttama. They held each other for a long time, while their bodies trembled and their eyes shed tears of joy. Dhruva's mother, Sunīti, touched his tender body and embraced him tightly, quickly forgetting the pain of long separation. Her eyes poured forth tears of affection, which drenched her breast together with a sudden flow of milk. All who lived in the palace were thrilled to see that wonderful scene of a mother meeting her lost son. They told Queen Sunīti, "O Mahārāṇī! Look at the exalted glory of your son! His long awaited return has dispelled all our sorrow. You were granted the opportunity to see him again today due to the result of pious activities performed in many lifetimes. We are sure that this boy will become emperor. The Lord removes the sufferings of His devotees and you will be able to worship His lotus feet, which dispel all fears and grant the yogis, who worship Him, the power to conquer even invincible death. Indeed ,the Lord takes away the miseries of the devotees who take shelter of Him."

King Uttānapāda put Dhruva and his brother Uttama on the back of an elephant, which rode them to town in a great, jubilant procession. When the citizens came to know that Uttānapāda's son was coming, they became almost mad with joy and started preparing many auspicious celebrations. Everyone was very busy making beautiful decorations for the doors of all the buildings, along with collecting fruits, blossoms, young banana trees, mango twigs, beautiful cloths, garlands and valuable stones. They lined the streets with pots filled with water and lamps, all nicely arranged. They decorated all the palaces and main gates of the city with very attractive golden cloths. They sprayed sandalwood water on the yards, main roads, housetops, leisure places and lanes and displayed raw and puffed rice, grains, flowers, fruits, sweets, clothes, ornaments and *pūjā* articles. All the citizens became very happy as Prince Dhruva passed by. The ladies of the town, full of motherly affection, showered upon him white mustard seeds and grains, and offered him curd, water, *darbha* grass, flowers, fruits and many other gifts, along with innumerable blessings.

While the citizens sang captivating melodies, Dhruva entered the palace of his father, which was studded everywhere with precious gems. King Uttānapāda took great care of Dhruva, carefully nourishing him as though he were a god. The palace had beautiful ivory beds—white like milk, and decorated with gold and jewels—and precious seats with gold-leafed decorations. Everything was beautifully ornamented. The palace walls were studded with crystal-clear blue sapphires and had bas-reliefs of images of women holding brilliant lamps to illuminate the place. Near the palace lay a beautiful garden full of wonderful trees, where birds sang sweetly and bees, intoxicated with honey, buzzed around and around. In the middle of the garden was a small lake with steps that descended into water, glistening with diamonds. There were exotic white lilies and lotus flowers blossoming on the surface of the water. Swans, herons and other aquatic birds of much grace lithely moved around, which only served to enhance the beauty of the pond.

King Uttānapāda was astounded to see and hear the magnificent glories of his son Dhruva. When Dhruva came of age, the king consulted with his ministers and anointed him *Yuvarāja*

(Prince Regent), and was very happy to see the respect that all the citizens had for him. When the king became old, after pondering the meaning of *ātmā-tattva,* he detached himself from all material objects, such as the opulence of his kingdom and the association of his wives and children. He became a renunciate and left the palace alone and on foot.

Dhruva became a powerful king and married two brides. His first queen was Bhrami, daughter of King Śiśumāra, and the second was Ilā, the daughter of Vāyu. The first queen gave birth to two sons, Kalpa and Vatsara, while the second queen gave birth to one son, Utkala, and one beautiful daughter, who was a true jewel among women.

Dhruva's younger brother Uttama, the son of his stepmother, did not marry. One day he went to the Himalayas to hunt deer, and found himself caught in an ambush by the Yakṣas. He fought fiercely for some time, but he could not escape death and was finally killed by a powerful Yakṣa.

Upon receipt of the sad news of the gruesome killing of his younger brother by the Yakṣas, Dhruva felt bereaved and lamented his death. Thinking about the cruel act of the Yakṣas, he felt a fuming anger and said, "Ah, those swarthy Yakṣa warriors have shown their great prowess and manliness by attacking together one lone man and killing him mercilessly. They have become drunk with delusions of power, but now I will give them what they deserve." Thinking in this way, he ordered his servants to prepare his chariot called "The Victor" and set off hurriedly in the northern direction, toward the country of the Yakṣas.

Arriving near the Himalayan Mountains, Dhruva sighted the wonderful capital of the Yakṣas, Alakapuri, which was protected by an army of ghosts and goblins, followers of Śiva, who resided in the town. Approaching the city, Dhruva blew his conch-shell, the reverberations of which could be heard far and wide, striking fear into the hearts of the wives of the Yakṣas. Hearing this extraordinary sound, the powerful army (which belonged to Kuvera, the brother of Lord Śiva) tasted fear for the very first time, and became overcome by panic. Dhruva saw many angry Yakṣas running toward him with raised weapons, shouting, "Kill! Kill!" The great archer, Dhruva, looked at the marching Yakṣa army and, shooting three arrows at each enemy, he pierced their foreheads.

Seeing the uncommon valor of Dhruva, the Yakṣa army was taken aback. The soldiers began to think that they might not be able to overpower him and they hesitated for a moment. Like a trampled snake that springs up to bite, the Yakṣa army, hit by many arrows, sprang up with a loud roar, determined to kill. Dhruva shot six arrows at each soldier. In response to Dhruva's action, they hurled a shower of wooden clubs studded with iron nails at both him and his charioteer, followed by falchions, spears, axles, iron bars, swords and spears full of iron nails. All these different missiles fell ceaselessly like a rain shower, so much so that the mountain vista was obscured, as it might be during a rainstorm. So furious was the showering of weapons that Dhruva and his charioteer were no longer visible. The Siddhas from heaven were watching the great battle between Dhruva and the Yakṣa army with much amazement and exclaimed, "Oh see how Dhruva, the descendant of Manu, has been covered like the setting sun by the ocean of weapons of the Yakṣas! Now that he is completely submerged by this rain of darts, the Yakṣa army is cheering loudly as though triumphant."

But just as the sun breaks through the clouds and dispels

the fog, Dhruva's chariot again came into view, breaking through the mass of arrows. At that moment, the loud cheering of the Yakṣa army stopped as suddenly as it had started and they stood amazed while Dhruva, in their midst, ceaselessly challenged them. Like a mighty wind scatters the clouds, Dhruva poured arrows upon his enemies, making a fine dust of their weapons. Then, like a hailstorm lashing a mountainside, he fired off a storm of very sharp arrows that pierced their armored bodies. The battlefield was strewn with the limbs of the Yakṣas that had been cut by Dhruva's crescent-shaped arrows. There were heads decorated by beautiful earrings, thighs resembling nice palm trees, arms decorated with attractive bracelets, necks adorned by valuable gold chains, hands still wearing bangles, heads carrying crowns or turbans—an amazing and strangely decorated scene. Dhruva killed many Yakṣa warriors, and those who were still alive were either mutilated or fleeing from the battlefield, like elephants running for their lives before a lion. Very soon, Dhruva could not see even one enemy standing in arms—the town was completely deserted.

Although attracted by the beauty of the Yakṣa city, Dhruva did not venture into it. He was apprehensive of the profound silence, because he knew that the Yakṣas were great wizards; no one knows when they might perform some magic! Human beings cannot comprehend the mystical powers of the Yakṣas. After consulting with his charioteer, Dhruva waited with great vigilance, his eyes searching all directions, because the enemy could attack from any side, at any moment.

Suddenly a roaring, thundering noise broke the silence and, at the same time, a powerful blast of wind blew violently, shaking everything. Great columns of dust formed, the sky became filled with dense clouds and angry, zigzagging bolts of lightning flashed in rapid succession, causing all the living entities to cry out in fear and anguish. A heavy rain started to fall, but it was not made of water. Blood, mucus, pus, stool, urine and flesh descended from above, along with countless severed heads and bodies, all drenched in blood. This ghastly rain fell for some time. Then a mountain appeared in the sky, from which an avalanche of stones fell from every direction, together with clubs, maces, swords, flaming torches and innumerable other weapons.

Soon after, many different frightening visions appeared, so terrifying that they could drain all courage from anyone. A host of powerful snakes, hissing with a thunderous cry and emanating fire from their eyes, charged toward Dhruva. He was being attacked by groups of running, mad elephants, lions, tigers and other ferocious animals. A mighty swell of water, with many furious waves slashing and roaring, surged forward as if to submerge everything. It was like the inundation at the time of universal dissolution.

The cruel-natured Yakṣas were attempting to confuse Dhruva with black magic. Dhruva saw many astounding and frightening visions that bewildered him and made him feel discouraged. Then the *munis*, out of their mercy, approached Dhruva and, after praying for his well-being, said, "O Dhruva, son of Uttānapāda, destroy your enemies by means of the Name of Śrī Hari, Who carries the disc and takes away the sufferings of those who offer Him their obeisances. Merely by being pronounced or heard, that Holy Name easily rescues the *jīvās* in this world from the hands of death."

Dhruva could understand the solution suggested by the *ṛṣis*' words and, after performing *ācamana*, he fixed the *nārāyaṇa-astra* to his bow and fired it. As soon as he had done this, the illusions of the Yakṣas vanished, just as the dawning of knowledge dissipates the darkness of ignorance and anger. The *nārāyaṇa-astra* started to penetrate the enemies' army as swiftly as a flock of black swans enters a forest, loudly calling to each other. Many sharp arrows pierced every Yakṣa, causing panic and great anger. Like a beaten snake, lame with pain and fear and feeling its death approaching, raises its hood to attack the divine bird, Garuḍa, so too, the panicked and ailing Yakṣas, full of anger, came toward Dhruva with weapons raised. The Yakṣa army was again marching on the battlefield, but Dhruva killed many of them by striking blows to their arms, thighs, necks, abdomens, felling them to the ground. Those Yakṣas, who were killed by Dhruva's hand, reached a higher abode, just like the *brahmacārīs* and *sannyāsīs* who, by strictly observing rules of celibacy, enter the orbit of the sun to reside there by the strength of their *tapasya*.

Grandfather Manu observed that, in the course of the fierce fighting, the mighty Dhruva had also killed many innocent Yakṣas. So, full of pity toward them, he personally went to meet Dhruva on the battlefield, accompanied by many *ṛṣis*. Svāyambhuva Manu told Dhruva, "Dear Dhruva, your anger has driven you to kill many innocent Yakṣas, and this constitutes cruelty on your part. Anger is the very door that leads to hell. You should understand and avoid it. Your brother was killed by only one Yakṣa but, due to the vehemence of your wrath and violent behavior, you have unfairly destroyed great numbers of them. Only those who have an animalistic nature, fuelled by false identification with the body and a sense of possessiveness toward that which is related to the body, can hurt other living entities. Devotees and *sādhus* are not violent by nature, so you should never follow the path of violence, as it does not befit you. You should always meditate on

Śrī Hari only, forgetting all else. By means of worship, you have satisfied the Supreme Soul of all living entities, Who is very difficult to worship, and you have obtained a very exalted position, earning the praise of all the devotees of the Lord. You know very well what the behavior of a *sādhu* should be, so we are puzzled as to why you are still bent on committing violence.

"The Lord is the Supreme Soul of everyone and He is pleased with those who behave respectfully toward superiors, make friends with equals and show mercy to inferiors. When the Lord is pleased with someone, that person will not remain bound by the influence of the material nature, but will attain a spiritual position, where everything is comprised of happiness and bliss. Creation, maintenance and annihilation are a result of the action of the innumerable qualities and potencies of the Supreme Lord. The Lord is never ruled by the *guṇas*, but rather, as the creator of the material qualities, He utilizes them for His own purpose. The omnipotent Lord acts in inconceivable ways. Although He is not the doer, He acts and He destroys, without being the killer. The Lord is the form of Time Himself, without origin, without end and inexhaustible. He creates the living entities through the agency of other living entities and, in the same way, He creates the universe and destroys it through the agency of death. Therefore, He is known as the Destroyer. Time, in the form of death, has no enemies or friends. Just as the wind blows around dust and dry leaves, so time sweeps away all the living entities that are subject to *karma*. Omnipotent Time is situated in Himself, therefore He is neither inside nor outside the power of time, nor under the power of *karma*. To some, He gives untimely death; to others He gives protection. The *karma-mimaṁsaka* philosophers affirm that time gives only the result of *karma*. Atheists say that it is just the workings of Nature. Materialists say that it is only death. Astrologers say that it is destiny awarded by the stars and the planets. The Vatsayanaya Ṛṣis say that time only grants the results of the desires of the conditioned living entities. The Lord is unmanifest, omnipotent and self-existent. No one is higher than the Lord. Therefore, no one can really say or understand why He acts in one way or the other. Dear Dhruva, you should not think that the Yakṣas are actually responsible for the killing of your brother. Rather, it is the will of God that gives birth and death to the human beings. Although He creates, maintains and annihilates the world, He is never touched by these activities and never falls subject to the influence of material nature. Everything always remains under His control. In the eyes of the non-devotees, He is death and fear personified, but to the devotees He is seen as a most affectionate, powerful superior and protector. He is the Supreme Shelter of all the living entities of this world. You should take shelter in the Lord with all your heart. All the *devas*, beginning with Brahmā, worship the Lord, while completely taking shelter of His lotus feet and, according to His wishes, execute all the works necessary for the creation, maintenance and annihilation of the universe.

"Dear Dhruva, you know that, at the tender age of five, you left your own mother to go to the forest, driven by the pain caused by the harsh words of your stepmother. There, you pleased the Lord by your strong austerities and obtained a boon from Him. Just see how you obtained such an exalted position by the unlimited mercy of the Supreme Lord! Śrī Hari always resides in the hearts of those who treat other living entities in an amicable and friendly manner and who exhibit no partiality toward either enemies or friends. How is it possible then, for a devotee, who has fixed his mind on the service of the Lord, to see any difference between enemies and friends? If you constantly strive to cultivate great devotion to the Lord, devotion of an unconditional and undiminishing nature, you will very easily cut the bonds of ignorance based upon bodily identification, which cause one to make false differentiations between enemies and friends. Dear Dhruva, the *ṛṣis* and I bless you with all good fortune. Give up your anger, because it is definitely contrary to the proper method for attainment of the higher good. Just as the correct administration of a medicine will make a disease go away, knowledge of the *śāstras* enables one to renounce anger. Any person who falls subject to anger will cause great suffering to all living entities. Therefore an intelligent person, desirous of his own welfare, will never allow himself to be controlled by anger. I will also tell you something else, for your own benefit. To avenge the killing of your brother you have slaughtered many Yakṣas. This was an offense to Śiva's brother, Kuvera and, if you don't settle this problem with him, the situation will not bode well for you. Beware of the power of the *devas*, who may cause troubles to our dynasty! You should quickly approach Kuvera, offer him respects and please him with your prayers."

After receiving these instructions from his grandfather, Dhruva felt ashamed for what he had done, and offered obeisances and prayers to him. Pleased with Dhruva's prayers, Svāyambhuva Manu returned to his abode, accompanied by all the *ṛṣis*.

As suggested by his grandfather, Dhruva gave up his anger and refrained from further killing. Understanding Dhruva's change of heart, the lord of wealth, Kuvera, accompanied by his retinue and followers, who were singing and reciting hymns in praise of him, approached Dhruva. Kuvera saw Dhruva standing still with folded hands, and told him, "O descendant of the *kṣatriya* race, sinless Dhruva, I am very pleased with you. On the order of your grandfather, Manu, you have given up all enmity, which is a feat very difficult to accomplish. I do not consider you to be the killer of the Yakṣas, just as I do not consider them to be the killers of your brother, because it is only time which causes birth and death for all living entities. Surely any differentiation in this matter is derived from ignorance and will cause bondage and unlimited suffering. Being proud of one's body generates the tendency to discriminate between enemies and friends, but this idea is only temporary and valueless like a dream. Therefore, O Dhruva, you should learn to see how the Supreme Soul is in all the living entities. When you leave this place, you should worship the lotus feet of the Lord, Who, as the Supreme Soul of all living entities, is removing all their miseries through His inconceivable plans. O son of Uttānapāda, if you want to ask any boon of me, please ask without fear. We have heard that you have obtained the lotus feet of Śrī Padmānabha Hari. Therefore, without any doubt, you are already qualified to receive any blessing."

Encouraged to ask for a boon from Kuvera, Dhruva intelligently asked for a specific blessing: "O lord, if you wish to grant me a boon, please bless me that I will constantly remember Śrī Hari and, by this remembrance, I will be able to overcome illusion, which is so difficult to overcome." Kuvera, the son of Iḍaviḍā, was very pleased by Dhruva's prayer and promptly replied, "So be it." After granting this boon, Kuvera disappeared from that place, and Dhruva returned home. Arriving there, Maharaj Dhruva celebrated a grand ceremony, performing a *yajña* to please Śrī Hari, the Lord of all sacrifices, Who gives everyone the result of their own activities. He then distributed charity throughout his city.

Free from all material designations and full of unalloyed devotion to Śrī Hari, the infallible Supreme Soul, Dhruva could feel the presence of Śrī Hari in himself and in all living entities. All the citizens could see that Dhruva was a great devotee of the Lord. He was affectionate to the bona fide *brāhmaṇas* and merciful to the poor, so they considered him their protector and sustainer, like a father to them. Dhruva terminated the result of his pious activities by the enjoyment of material pleasure and he terminated any inauspicious reactions by practicing yoga and austerities, during the 36,000 years of his reign over the world. Dhruva ruled the kingdom with controlled senses and purified consciousness, seeing everything, from his own body to the whole universe, as a mere dream—a dream made of illusions, temporary in nature and ephemeral like the heavenly places. To fulfill his duties as king, he spent a long time in celebrating many kinds of sacrifices that award the results of *artha, kāma* and *dharma*. Finally, he decided to concentrate wholly on the worship of the Supreme Lord and, after entrusting the burden of the kingdom to his son, he went to Badarikāśrama. Considering the temporary nature of the body and the things connected to it (such as the relationship with wives, sons, friends and well-wishers) and of his kingly paraphernalia (such as his army, opulent treasury, palaces, attractive gardens and strolling places), which were all in a great kingdom extending throughout the land to the shores of the sea, he could understand that all this could be taken away at any moment, by the influence of time. With this in mind, he gave all these things up, then and there.

In Badarikāśrama, Dhruva bathed with holy water, purified his senses and then sat down to perform yoga, using his mind to withdraw the senses from the sense objects. He then started to meditate on the gross elements of the Universal Form of the Supreme Lord. Constantly engaged in this meditation, he attained firm faith in God and reached *samādhi,* relinquishing all thoughts of the material body. Dhruva's devotion surged toward the Lord like a mighty river. Tears of joy rolled from his eyes and, while experiencing the happiness of love, his heart melted and ecstatic symptoms appeared on his body. After losing all bodily consciousness in this way, he saw a wonderful glowing light similar to the moon, emanating from a beautiful airplane that descended from the sky. Inside the airplane, he could see two handsome, dark-colored divine beings of youthful appearance, with four arms, holding maces, who were wearing beautiful clothes and were decorated with many ornaments, such as crowns, gold chains, earrings and so on.

Dhruva felt very excited because he could see that they were servants of Lord Uttamaśloka, dear associates of Śrī Hari, and he became confused about how best to welcome them. Rising from his *āsana* with folded hands, he simply uttered the Name of the Lord and offered obeisances to them. Sunanda and Nanda, the two dear-most companions of Śrī Krishna, who always meditate on His lotus feet, stood respectfully with folded hands and, with smiling faces, they politely addressed Dhruva by invoking the Lord's Name. The dear companions of Lord Nārāyaṇa said, "O King, all good fortune to you! Please listen attentively to our words. When you were only a five-year-old boy, you pleased the Lord and sustainer of the universe by your austerities. We are His servants. Now we shall take you to the lotus feet of the Lord. We have come here for this purpose. You have obtained Śrī Vishnu's planet, which is very difficult to reach. Even the Seven Ṛṣis can only contemplate it without actually being able to reach it. All the stars and planets, the sun and the moon are always circumambulating that planet. Now you will reach it. O Dhruva! No one could ever reach that position before you, not even your father or your ancestors. Everyone will honor you for this glorious achievement. Please ascend to Vishnu's planet, O immortal one! This nice airplane has been sent for you by the Lord. Please board it."

Dhruva listened to the nectarean speech of the two dearmost companions of the Lord of Vaikuṇṭha and felt very happy. Then, he bathed and performed his ritual duties, offering his respects to the sages and begging for their blessings. Finally, he circumambulated the beautiful airplane and worshiped it with fragrant flowers and other articles and similarly honored the two divine messengers. As he approached the airplane, his body became very brilliant. At that time, he could see death itself approaching and, fearlessly, he stepped on its head to get on the airplane, thus conquering death itself.

Acclamations were heard from all directions, together with the sound of drums, conch-shells and other musical instruments, while a shower of flowers fell from the sky. Dhruva was about to leave for Vishnu's abode, when, suddenly, he thought of his mother and felt sorrowful, knowing that he was about to leave for heaven without her. The two companions of the Lord could understand the feelings in his heart and said, "O King, behold! Your mother is riding in another airplane in front of us." Amazed, Dhruva saw the airplane and all his worries were vanquished.

While Dhruva was traveling upward to heaven, the *devas*, who were hovering in airplanes singing his glories, showered him with a rain of beautiful flowers. Gradually, Dhruva could see all the planets and, crossing them without difficulty, he reached the planet of Vishnu, which is above the three worlds and the constellation of the Seven Ṛṣis. That planet is always self-effulgent and illuminates all the planets beneath it, with its light. It is the supreme abode destined for those saints who are always engaged in working for the actual welfare of others. Those who are peaceful, equal to everyone, pure and always engaged in helping other living entities to serve Śrī Hari, easily reach that planet. It can be attained without difficulty by those who take pleasure in the soul and consider Śrī Krishna to be their dearest friend and protector. Just as oxen tread around the pole to which they are tied, all constellations revolve forcefully, without ever stopping, around Dhruvaloka. The son of Uttānapāda thus obtained the topmost position in all the three worlds.

Once, Devārṣi Nārada was present at an assembly of kings, who were performing a *yajña*, and he began to narrate the glories of the great devotee, Dhruva, all the while playing on his vina. He said, "Dhruva, the son of chaste Sunīti, by the power of his austerities, obtained a result which could never be obtained by the great *ṛṣis*, what to speak of the kings of this mundane world. At the age of five, Dhruva went to the forest, driven by the pain inflicted upon him by the harsh words of his stepmother and, by following my instructions, he was able to attract, by his devotion, the invincible Lord Śrī Hari. This is because the unconquerable Lord is always conquered by His devotee. A mere boy, of only five years, Dhruva could reach that supreme position after having worshiped the Lord for just a few days, while no other *kṣatriya* could even aspire to such an elevated platform, even after trying for many, many years."

The Holy Life of Prahlad

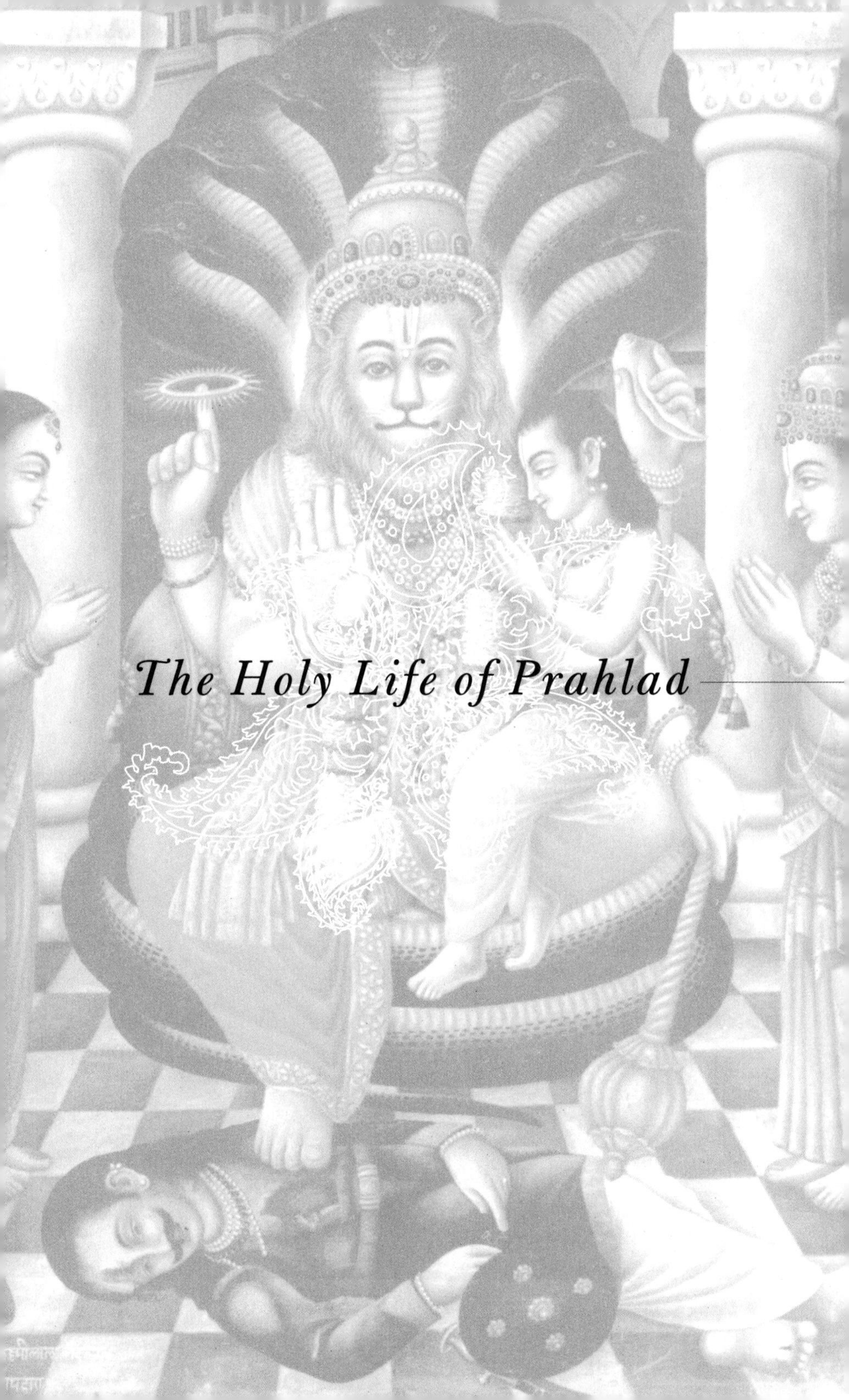

The Holy Life of Prahlad

the BIRTH of HIRANYAKASIPU

Once, in the course of their travels around the three worlds, the four sages born from the mind of Brahmā (Sanaka, Sanandana, Sanātana and Sanat-kumāra) arrived unannounced at Vaikuṇṭha, the residence of the Supreme Lord. Although the Four Kumāras are actually very old, their appearance is like that of small children and they travel around naked.

It so happened that the two gatekeepers of Vaikuṇṭha, Jaya and Vijaya, saw the Four Kumāras approaching. Thinking them to be ordinary children, they prevented the sages from entering Vaikuṇṭha, addressing them thus: "Where have you come from? Are you unaware that no one can enter here without prior permission?"

Although the Four Kumāras repeatedly tried to enter Vaikuṇṭha, Jaya and Vijaya kept turning them away. Finally, becoming angry, the Four Kumāras cursed the gatekeepers, exclaiming, "You rascals! You are prohibiting us from entering without exercising proper discrimination and out of pride only. In the abode of the Lord, the qualities of ignorance and passion cannot exist. Thus you are not qualified to reside at the lotus feet of Lord Madhusūdana. We therefore curse you to fall down from this place and to take birth as demons with material bodies."

Reeling from the blow of the sages' powerful curse, Jaya and Vijaya immediately fell from their exalted position. Seeing their miserable plight, the Four Kumāras took pity on them and promised them that, after three lifetimes, they would be relieved from the effect of their curse.

In their first birth, Jaya and Vijaya became the sons of Diti, the matriarch of the demonic race. The elder son was named Hiraëyakaçipu and the younger son was named Hiraṇyakṣa. Both commanded the respect of all the demons.

When the Lord descended as His boar-incarnation, Varāha Deva, to rescue the falling earth by lifting it with His tusks, Hiraṇyakṣa violently opposed Him. After a fierce battle, Lord Varaha ended Hiraṇyakṣa's life. When Hiraṇyakaśipu heard the news of the death of his brother, he became deeply aggrieved. He bit his lips in a rage of terrible anger and the smoke from his burning eyes clouded the sky. With grinding teeth and frowning brows, he appeared extremely frightening. While brandishing his *śūla* weapon, he addressed the demons as follows:

"O my fellow demons! All of you prepare immediately to take action according to my instructions. Do not hesitate! Some insignificant enemies have killed my beloved younger brother, Hiraṇyakṣa, who always loved me dearly. It is said that Lord Śrī Hari is impartial to one and all. Yet it seems that He is helping our enemies due to the demigods having offered Him some worship. I therefore declare that the Lord does not possess equal vision.

Although God is pure and powerful, after taking the form of the boar, Varaha Deva, His mind became unsteady like that of a child. With this weapon I shall cut off the head of Vishnu and then I shall offer the blood gushing from His neck to my brother, Hiraṇyakṣa, who was very fond of drinking blood. Only then will the pain in my heart be relieved."

Fuming with anger, Hiraṇyakaśipu paused briefly, and then continued addressing the demons. "When a tree is cut at the root, all the branches and leaves will naturally dry up. In the same way, if my enemy Vishnu is killed, all the demigods will perish because Vishnu is their life and soul. Until I succeed in killing Vishnu, you should persist in killing all those who perform acts of spiritual virtue such as austerities, worship, sacrifices, study of the *Vedas*, the making of vows and giving in charity. You should also kill all those, such as *brāhmaṇas*, *kṣatriyas* and other human beings, who sincerely follow their religious duty in accordance with the principles of *dharma*. Vishnu is the beneficiary of sacrifices performed by the *brāhmaṇas*. Vishnu is well known as the supreme shelter of *dharma* and the Lord of sacrifice, Yajñesvara. The demigods take their share of the sacrifice only after He has. If you kill the *brāhmaṇas*, all sacrifices and other religious activities will be stopped. As a result, Vishnu will become weak and will finally be destroyed. The cows survive by eating grass and they supply ghee from their milk. The *brāhmaṇas* perform their sacrificial offerings to Vishnu by using *ghee* and Vedic mantras. Hereby the strength and power of the Lord is nourished. Therefore, you should destroy all the trees and plants that can be eaten by the cows and torch all the places where you see cows, *brāhmaṇas*, the *Vedas* or people following the system of *varṇāśrama* as recommended by the *Vedas*."

As it is the intrinsic nature of demons to take pleasure in violence and destruction, they accepted the orders of Hiraṇyakaśipu with great enthusiasm and respect. Like madmen, they began to harass the people. In a rage of destruction, they burned to ashes cities, villages, cowsheds, gardens, granaries, agricultural fields, forests, the *āśramas* of the sages, the dwellings of farmers, the grazing fields in the valleys between the mountains, the capitals of kingdoms and everything else that came to their minds. Some of the demons demolished bridges, buildings and city gates with their iron spears and torched them after they had finished. Some felled mango trees, jackfruit trees and other valuable fruit trees with their axes, cutting them to pieces. Other demons took up flaming torches and ran around in wild abandon, burning residential houses and other buildings to the ground. In this way, the demoniac servants of Hiraṇyakaśipu created a non-stop and gravely serious disturbance for all the people, so much so, that the performance of *yajñas* and other pious activities became extremely difficult, if not impossible. Unable to receive their share of the sacrifices, the demigods left the heavenly realm (Svargaloka) and began to move about clandestinely in this world.

the INSTRUCTIONS of HIRANYAKASIPU

Meanwhile Bhānu, the wife of Hiraṇyakṣa, was experiencing great suffering due to separation from her husband. Feeling helpless in her grief, she loudly lamented her sudden widowhood. The sons of Hiraṇyakṣa were also desperately grieving the death of their father.

After completing his brother's funeral ceremonies, Hiraṇyakaśipu tried to pacify them. With a comforting voice he spoke:

"O sister-in-law, dear to me like a mother! O children of my valiant brother! You should not grieve like this for such a great hero, who has surrendered his life without fear after an open fight on the battlefield. Warriors and heroes actually aspire to such an honorable death, considering it to be their most desirable achievement.

"In this world, we are like travelers, who stop for some time at a resting place on the road. Why should we be so aggrieved to leave this place? We all come from different places, we meet for a short time and again leave, each to a different destination. All living entities encounter each other according to their previous *karma* and, due to the result of previous activities, they are separated again and proceed on to different destinations, in many directions.

"Actually, the original form of the self is the soul, which is different from the body and is never destroyed like the body. The soul is eternal and is not subject to change or transformation. He is pure, omnipresent and omniscient. The soul does not actually enjoy or suffer material experiences, but experiences pleasure or suffering due to being covered and contaminated by ignorance. For this reason only, the self loses his original knowledge and feels loss and lamentation. When the water of a lake trembles, the trees standing on the bank of the lake also seem to tremble in the reflection of the water. Likewise, someone who is moving around will see the world around him as moving. Consequently, the mind becomes agitated by the action of the threefold qualities of material nature [the *guṇas*] but this is actually due to the material contamination of identifying oneself with the mind and body.

"To those who identify with their bodies, pleasure means

obtaining what is dear to or desired by the body and avoiding what they do not like, while suffering is the inability to get what the body likes or having to experience what the body does not like. This identification with the material body is the prime cause of *karma*, which forces us to take birth in a womb and begin the process of suffering. *Karma* [selfish activity] is the root cause of material existence, creating birth, death, ignorance, anxiety and many other sufferings and ignominies.

"Although sometimes, in the cycle of *karma,* we may gain some understanding and knowledge, we unfortunately tend to forget it all as our material sojourn evolves. This is nicely illustrated in a conversation held between Yamarāja, the lord of death, and the relatives of a man recently deceased. Please listen as I narrate this ancient story to you:

In the kingdom of Uśinara there lived a famous king named Suyajña. One day, his enemies attacked his kingdom and the king set out with his army to engage in battle. However, in the great fight that ensued, the king was killed. At the news of his death, all the citizens of Uśinara were grief-stricken.

The body of the king was lying on the battlefield, pierced by many sharp arrows and drenched in blood. Yet, in spite of his many wounds, scattered hair and dull eyes, the king's face still displayed his immense feelings of wrath. His decorated armor was torn to pieces, his jewels and ornaments were scattered all around and the dust of the battlefield clouded the luster of his face. Even his hands had been horribly severed from his body and were strewn about in different places, still grasping weapons that gleamed in the sunlight. When the king's family arrived on the scene, they sat down around the dead body and started to cry. The queens beat their chests without cessation and threw themselves at his feet: 'O lord of our lives, where have you gone? How can we survive without you?' The poor ladies, sunk in desperation, raised a loud wail of lamentation. The torrents of tears that poured from their eyes displayed their endless sorrow and bathed the king's feet, while the red kuṅkuma smeared on their breasts only served to increase the intense drama of the scene.

No longer taking pleasure in elegance and beauty, the queens loosened their nicely arranged hair, tossing and breaking their expensive ornaments. Now that their husband was dead, they felt that nothing mattered any more. Their husband had been their only pleasure and hope and the loss of him left them feeling desperate. Their woeful lamentation filled all the living entities with sorrow. They addressed their dead husband by saying:

'O lord and master, how can we bear to see you in this situation? God is so cruel! He has taken away our support and protection, our husband who was dearer to us than life itself. O lord of our lives, our husband! You now lie before us—you, who were once the maintainer of all the people of Uśinara. You used to make them all happy, but today you have made them most unhappy with your death. O protector of the land, O great warrior, you were our best friend, always dutiful and concerned about our welfare. How can we maintain our life without you? O lord, please also take us with you, wherever you are going, so that we may serve your feet there.'

When the undertakers came to take the body for cremation, the queens caught hold of it with a very tight embrace, and their lamentation grew even louder. The sunset had passed, but they would not leave their husband's body. All this crying and lamentation finally came to the ears of Yamarāja in his abode. It disturbed his mind to such an extent that he resolved to take the form of a boy to go and speak with the king's family personally. After reaching there, he addressed them thus:

'This is truly amazing! You are grown-up people—older than me—but here I see you crying and lamenting without good reason. You have always seen birth and death occurring around you, yet how great is the attachment you seem to have developed! You should know that all human beings come from an unknown place and again they will have to depart to the unknown. It is unavoidable, since all those who are born must one day die. So why do you continue to lament?

'Although I am just a child, I understand this better than you. Taking birth from our parents, we have fallen prey to these material forms that are full of misery. We seem helpless and without protection. Yet there is someone who protects us, otherwise we would not have been able to survive in our mother's womb, and we could easily have been devoured by some ferocious animals. O ignorant people! Our real protector is the Supreme Lord, by Whose will alone this world is created, protected and destroyed. Compared to Him, all moving and non-moving living entities are very insignificant. He has full power to create and destroy. Everything is possible for Him. If someone inadvertently drops an object on the road while traveling, by the

protection of God no one will touch it and he will be able to find it again. Yet, without the protection of God, even if we keep our property locked up and well guarded inside our house, we will lose it and it will be destroyed..

'By the merciful glance of the Lord, one can survive even after becoming lost in a jungle, in spite of being alone and helpless. Each individual obtains a body according to his previous karma and, when that karma is finished, the body will vanish. What is the value of this body? This body continuously suffers the six changes of birth, growth, conservation, loss, decline and destruction.

'The soul resides within the gross and subtle bodies, but is not born. It does not undergo the same changes as the body, because the nature of the self is very different from that of the body. As the owner of a house is different from the house itself, the self is the proprietor of the body and is therefore different from it. It is only out of attachment that people think, 'I am this material body'. Earth, water, fire and air form the human body in the beginning, yet, by the laws of nature, they will dissolve and the body will disappear. The soul, however, is never destroyed.

'You may find it difficult to understand how the self is separate from the body, because you are accustomed to seeing them together. I can enlighten you with the example of fire. Fire is inherent in wood, but only during combustion can we easily observe the difference in the nature of wood and of fire, which is powerful and brilliant. Similarly the soul resides in the body and senses of the living entity, but we can observe that he is different from them.

'O foolish people! You are lamenting so much for this body, even while it is lying dead in front of you. It has not

gone to some other place. Why are you lamenting? This person used to listen and reply to your words, but now he does not. Please do not lament for that. The person who was actually listening and replying was never seen by anyone. The body you used to see is still here for you to see. It is exactly the same body as before. Therefore, there is no need to lament for the body.

'The soul animates and protects the body but, if the body can no longer listen and reply, it means that it is devoid of consciousness. The soul interacts with all objects through the senses, but he is different from the senses of the body. He is actually made of consciousness only. The five gross elements and the ten sense organs form the gross body, which covers the subtle body, made of mind, intellect and ego, and the soul relates to all these things by acting in ways both good and bad. This understanding is possible for those who perform worship of God.

'As long as the ātmā is related to the subtle body, it is bound by karma. From these ties of ignorance and forgetfulness comes the mistaken identification with the body and, subsequently, all suffering. We wrongly believe that whatever we get from the three guṇas is permanent. If we fantasize at night about being a king, enjoying a king's opulence and pleasures, our projections are unreal. When we have dreams of sexual activity, our experience is illusory and, in the same way, enjoying the senses in this world is not a real experience. The soul is eternal and the body is not, therefore there is no need to lament. Those who have no self-realization cannot do anything else but lament, this being their very nature.

'O queens, once upon a time there was a kuliṅga bird, who, just like you, was lamenting the loss of his wife. A hunter was traveling here and there in the forest and, wherever he saw some birds, he would spread out his net to capture and kill them, sometimes attracting them with bait. One day, by God's arrangement, while he was walking in the forest, the hunter saw a pair of kuliṅga birds, who were husband and wife. He put some of their favorite food inside the net and waited, hidden from their view.

'The female kuliṅga bird saw the very palatable food and became immediately attracted, but then she realized that she was caught in a net and began to struggle and cry, being terribly frightened. Although aggrieved at his wife's plight, the kuliṅga male was unable to rescue her, so he also started to lament very pitifully out of his love for her:

'"How cruel is Destiny! How cruel is the law of creation! After falling into this dangerous trap, my wife is crying out for me. What benefit can Destiny obtain from the death of my beloved? O cruel Fate, after taking my wife, who is the better half of my body, you should take me also! Without my beloved, why should I carry on living? Alas! Alas! Our small children are in the nest, awaiting their mother and starving without food. They do not even have any feathers yet. How will I be able to take care of these orphaned children without the help of their mother?"

'Desperate due to the impending death of his wife, the kuliṅga bird was crying like this, when, by the power of Time, the hunter approached him and shot him with an arrow, killing him as well.

'O foolish queens, you are also deprived of understanding, much like this kuliṅga bird, who could not see

his own death approaching. Even if you continued to lament for one hundred years, you would not be able to get your husband back.'"

After narrating this story about Yamarāja, Hiraṇyakaśipu concluded, "O wife and sons of my dear brother, the wives and relatives of King Suyajña were amazed at these instructions of Yama in the form of a boy, and they realized that all material things are temporary. Nothing can always remain as we see it now. After talking with them, Yama went away and the relatives of Suyajña completed the funeral ceremonies for the departed soul. In the same way, you should not lament too much for yourselves or for others. Who are these people for whom we are lamenting? What is there which we can call our own? All these considerations are due to ignorance and attachment to the body, and nothing else."

After hearing these instructions, Diti for some time forgot to lament for her dead son.

the TAPASYA of HIRANYAKASIPU

The lord of the Daityas, the terrible Hiraṇyakaśipu, wanted to become immortal, free from old age and invincible in all the three worlds. To attain his goal, he went to a cave in Mandara Mountain, and performed a great penance by standing still on his two big toes, while keeping his hands stretched toward the sky, his whole body straight like a stick.

Due to the force of his penance, a bright light emanated from Hiraṇyakaśipu's body. All the demigods were afraid of Hiraṇyakaśipu, and consequently they had been hiding here and there.

When they saw that Hiraṇyakaśipu was engaged in penance in a secluded place, they felt relieved and went back to their own palaces, convinced that there was no more cause for fear.

However, as a result of the terrible austerities of Hiraṇyakaśipu, fire and smoke started to emanate from his head, which scorched all the living entities in the lower and higher planetary systems. All the rivers and oceans became disturbed. The mountains, islands and continents started to shake. The planets and stars became unsteady and all the directions were filled with the burning radiance of Hiraṇyakaśipu's penance.

Because of the intolerable fire of that great *tapasya*, all the demigods fled from Svargaloka and approached Brahmāloka to pray to Brahmā to protect them from their fears. After offering prayers, they said:

"O master of the universe, O protector of everyone! This Hiraṇyakaśipu, lord of the demons, is performing a terrible penance. The power of his *tapasya* is forcing us out of Svargaloka. Please help and protect us, as we are your servants and worshipers. If you wish to protect your servants before they are destroyed, please stop Hiraṇyakaśipu from his *tapasya*, which is destroying the whole world.

"Hiraṇyakaśipu is engaged in this penance because he wants to obtain a boon; it is not impossible for you to grant him his wish. Although you know everything, we want to inform you about his desire, as we have understood it.

"Hiraṇyakaśipu is thinking, 'By my *tapasya*, I wish to obtain a position like that of Brahmā, who became the creator of the universe and is worshiped by everyone. The position of Brahmā is greater than that of any king, even Indra. I want the topmost position in Satyaloka. Since time is eternal and the soul is also eternal, I do not care how many lifetimes of penance I shall have to

Hiranyakasipu performs tapasya

undergo in order to attain this position, according to my desire. When I obtain sufficient power, I shall change the rules of this world. At the end of the *kalpa* [a day of Brahmā], the whole universe will be destroyed, including the Vaiṣṇavas. Therefore, I am not interested in any position lower than Brahmā's.'

"Now, Hiraṇyakaśipu has begun this great *tapasya* with the intention of obtaining your post. You are the lord of the three worlds, so please do whatever is necessary to solve this problem. This is our prayer. O creator and protector of the world! Your existence is the cause of pleasure, opulence, welfare and happiness for the cows and *brāhmaṇas*. If Hiraṇyakaśipu attains your position, all these things will be destroyed."

The demigods concluded their prayers, and Lord Brahmā, accompanied by all the sages, such as Bhṛgu, Dakṣa and others, departed to the hermitage of Hiraṇyakaśipu.

Meanwhile, Hiraṇyakaśipu had been performing penance for a very long time in the same position without ever moving, so much so that an anthill, upon which grass and reeds were growing, had covered his body. Ants had eaten his body to such an extent that the skin, flesh and blood had disappeared, leaving only bones.

Riding on his swan carrier, Brahmā arrived at the spot, but he could not see Hiraṇyakaśipu. Like the sun covered by clouds, Hiraṇyakaśipu's body was hidden, and Brahmā had to look very carefully. When he finally spotted him, he was amazed and addressed Hiraṇyakaśipu with a smile:

"O son of Kaśyapa, please arise. May you be blessed. Your *tapasya* has been successful and I have come to offer you a boon. Please ask for whatever you may desire. I am truly astounded to see your great penance. Ants have eaten your body and you have been able to retain your life in your bones only. In the past, not even Bhṛgu and the other *ṛṣis* were ever able to perform such a severe penance and in the future no one else will be able to do the same. Who could survive like you, without taking even water for one hundred years of the demigods?[1] O son of Diti, whatever was impossible for the *ṛṣis* you have successfully performed, and I have been attracted by your *tapasya*. O greatest among the *asuras*! For this reason I am ready to offer you the boon that you desire. Meeting with an immortal cannot be fruitless, so you may now ask whatever you like of me."

After saying this, Brahmā poured water from his divine *kamaṇḍalu* (water pot) onto the bones of Hiraṇyakaśipu, immediately transforming them into a new body, perfectly strong and youthful, powerful like lightning, with a beautiful golden complexion. Hiraṇyakaśipu emerged from the anthill and the cluster of reeds in the same way that fire rises from wood. Directly before him he could see Brahmā on his swan airplane, and tears of joy began to roll down from his eyes. He prostrated himself on the ground to offer his obeisances and, with his hair standing on end and in a faltering voice, he started to speak.

1. One of our Earth years constitutes only one day for the demigods. All the yearly pūjā festivals are therefore occurring every day for the demigods.

HIRANYAKASIPU OFFERS PRAYERS *to* BRAHMA *and* ASKS *for a* BOON

Hiraṇyakaśipu said, "At the end of the *kalpa*, when the destruction of the universe arrives, all the worlds, except the self-effulgent planets, enter into complete darkness. Then the creator, utilizing the three qualities of material nature [*guṇas*], again manifests the world. To that supreme personality, who creates, maintains and destroys the universe and is the shelter of the *guṇas*, I am offering my obeisances.

"You are the cause of the first manifestation of the universe, the form of knowledge and science, who manifests through the action and transformations of the life force, senses, mind and intellect. I offer you my respect.

"You are the supreme living entity, the protector of this world and the universal form of all living entities—therefore you are called Prajāpati, the lord and protector of all creatures and their original power of consciousness. You are also the protector of the mind and senses. O great personality, you are the lord of the objects of the senses [smell, taste, form, touch, and sound], the five gross elements [earth, water, fire, air and space] and all the qualities and desires.

"You are the personification of the *Ṛg*, *Sama* and *Yajur Vedas*. You manifest the followers of the three *Vedas* and the authorities on the *Atharva Veda*. All sacrifices, knowledge and paraphernalia used in the rituals of the ritviks, such as the fire sacrifice [*agnihotra*], are manifested by you alone.

"You are the life and soul of those who know *ātmā*, the self. You are without beginning, beyond all time and space. You are omnipresent, omniscient, the soul residing in the heart of every living entity. You are the eternally conscious personality who fixes the exact lifespan of all living entities, by counting even the smallest fraction of time and then taking their life when their moment has come. But you never change. You are unborn, the supreme controller of all living entities, their life and protector.

"Everything in this universe, all the good and bad things, the earth and the oceans, all are contained in you and are non-different from you. The *Vedas*, the Upaniṣads and all other Vedic literatures emanate from your body. You are the supreme reality, Hiranyagarbha, from whose navel the golden lotus sprouts. You are beyond the three *guṇas*.

"O powerful lord! Although you always reside in the greatest transcendental abode, you externally display the great form of Virāṭa-rūpa [the Universal Form], made of all the elements, objects of sense perception, senses, life force and mind. Although you manifest all this, you are personally beyond the reach of the senses.

"You are the supreme and oldest personality, the supreme soul living in the heart of every creature, unlimited, imperishable and omnipresent throughout the universe. I offer my obeisances to this Supreme Lord, who is always accompanied by His three energies: *antaraṅgā-śakti* [internal potency], *bahiraṅgā-śakti* [external potency] and *taṭasthā-śakti* [marginal potency].

"O lord! If you wish to fulfill my desire for a boon, then please grant this to me: grant that I shall not be killed by any of the living entities created by you, that I shall not be killed indoors or outdoors and that I shall not be killed during the day or the night. I shall not be killed by you, Rudra, or any other demigod or creature, or by any weapon. I shall not be killed on the ground or in the sky nor shall any human being or any animal such as a tiger or others kill me. Any living entity, inert matter, demigod, demon or great snake shall not kill me. Please grant that I shall not be killed by any of these.

"O lord! No one can oppose you in battle and you are the lord of all living entities and all rulers, so please give me this same position. Please grant me the eight *siddhis* [mystic perfections of yoga] and whatever results can be obtained by the practice of *tapasya* and yoga."

After listening to the prayers and requests of Hiraṇyakaśipu, Brahmā replied, "Dear son, I am now giving you whatever boon you have requested from me, although it is actually rare and difficult to obtain for anyone."

Then Brahmā, being worshiped by the king of the *asuras*, Hiraṇyakaśipu, and accompanied by the hymns of the *ṛṣis*, returned to his own abode.

By the blessing of Brahmā, Hiraṇyakaśipu had obtained all the boons he requested, as well as a very strong and powerful golden body. He then remembered the slaying of his brother and immediately felt great hatred toward Vishnu. This great *asura* became the supreme ruler of the other *asuras*, the demigods and human beings along with their kings. He also became the ruler of the Gandharvas, Nagas, Siddhas, Garuḍas, Cāraṇas, Vidyādharas, Ṛṣis, Yama and his followers, the Pitṛs, Manu, the Yakṣas, Rākṣasas, Piśācas, Pretas, Bhūtas (ghosts and devils) and all other living entities. After conquering their lords and kings, he took from them their powers and positions, and became the supreme personality in the three planetary systems of Svarga, Martya and Patala.

He established the beautiful palace of Indra as his residence, surrounded by Nandana Kanana Park, built by the architect of the demigods Viśvakarma, and lived there in great opulence. The palace sparkled with the light of innumerable priceless jewels. The stairs were studded with a copper-red gemstone called *padmarāga* (rubies), the floors were set with green *marakata* gems (emeralds) brought from Singhal Desh (China). The walls were decorated with crystals; the pillars were constructed with *vaidūrya-maṇi* (a valuable type of stone) of mixed black and yellow color. The light of the sun and the moon reflected by these gemstones created a wonderful brilliance.

The furniture of the palace was made with *padmarāga-maṇi*, all the beds were decorated with pearls and the gem called *dugdha-phena-nibha*. The palace resounded with attractive music created by the tinkling of the ornaments of beautiful and intelligent women who walked about discreetly while contemplating their own charming faces mirrored in the gems. Hiraṇyakaśipu lived in this wonderful abode of perfection, Mahendra Bhavana, after chasing out the demigods who loved it so dearly.

After assuming the post of supreme emperor of the universe, Hiraṇyakaśipu always resided at the palace of Indra. He would drink very strong wine and his copper-red eyes would roll around as if in anger. Because he possessed all the powers of *tapasya* and yoga, all the demigods, except Brahmā, Vishnu and Śiva, were forced to come forward and offer him garlands, worship and prostrated obeisances.

By dint of his enormous power, Hiraṇyakaśipu had conquered the kingdom of heaven, Svarga Rājya, and, because they feared him, all the Gandharvas, Siddhas, Vidyādharas, Apsarās and even Viśvāvasu, Tumburu, Nārada and other *ṛṣis* were engaged in singing his glories for his pleasure.

All the members of the *varṇas* (*brāhmaṇas*, *kṣatriyas*, *vaiśyas* and *śūdras*) and the *āśramas* (*brahmacārīs*, *gṛhasthas*, *vanacārīs* and *sannyāsīs*) offered gifts and sacrifices to him. Yet all this worship was rendered out of fear only. So great was his power and the fear he inspired that the fields started to produce foods spontaneously without being cultivated, much like the wish-fulfilling cow, *kāma-dhenu*. The sky was always clear and beautifully decorated with stars, only out of fear of Hiraṇyakaśipu. In the same way, the seven oceans—the Salty Ocean, the Sugarcane Juice Ocean, the Wine Ocean, the Ghee Ocean, the Milk Ocean, the Yogurt Ocean and the Nectar Ocean—and their wives (the Rivers) continuously offered many jewels to the demons by presenting them with their waves. The valleys between the hills were his playgrounds and, out of fear, all the trees were producing fruits throughout all six seasons of the year.

Hiraṇyakaśipu forcibly wrested the rain potency from Indra, the air potency from Vāyu, the fire potency from Agni and, after assuming the powers of all the demigods, lords and rulers, rendered them all powerless. Hiraṇyakaśipu was the invincible supreme ruler, but because he was not able to control his own senses—even after enjoying whatever he wished—he still could not find satisfaction. After enjoying all possible opulence he began to indulge in whatever is prohibited by the *śāstras*. He wasted so much time in this way that Sanaka and the other *ṛṣis* cursed him for it.

Oppressed by the cruelty of Hiraṇyakaśipu's rule, all the living entities and their lords, the demigods, approached Lord Vishnu, having decided to seek His shelter. Neglecting sleep, controlling their minds and senses and getting nourishment just from the air, all the demigods began to worship the Supreme Lord. They offered their obeisances to the Lord by facing the direction of His eternal abode, that place where renounced souls can remain eternally after having reached there.

At that time they heard a divine voice emanating from the sky that said, "Do not worry. O best of the learned sages, you need not fear. You are blessed. All living entities will obtain the fulfillment of their desires by meeting Me. I have seen the disturbance caused by the demon Hiraṇyakaśipu and I will arrange a suitable punishment for him. Because he has disturbed the demigods, *Vedas*, cows, *brāhmaṇas*, Vaiṣṇavas, *dharma* and Myself, his destruction will come about in the near future. Please wait patiently for the proper time. When this demon begins to harass his own son, Prahlad, who is a great soul, peaceful and benevolent to all, I shall destroy Hiraṇyakaśipu, even though he is protected by the boon of Brahmā. I can tolerate many things, but I cannot tolerate seeing the suffering of My devotee."

After hearing the voice of Lord Vishnu, all the *devas* who were residents of Svargaloka offered obeisances to Him and became pacified, convinced that the demon would be killed very soon.

The lord of the demons, Hiraṇyakaśipu, had four very powerful sons, named Prahlad, Anuhlad, Sanhlad and Ahlad. Among these four, Prahlad was the greatest. He always offered affection and respect to the devotees and he possessed all the good qualities of a *brāhmaṇa*: he was honest, good in character, truthful and self-controlled. Just like *Paramātmā*, he was the dearest friend of all living entities. He always respected his superiors by offering service and obeisances, considering himself to be their servant. To the helpless he was kind and loving like a father, and to those who were older than him, he offered affection and respect like a brother. He always offered the same respect he had for the Lord to his *dīkṣā* and *śikṣā* gurus, as well as to his godbrothers. Although he was very learned, wealthy, handsome, expert and great in all respects, he was also free from pride.

Although Prahlad had taken birth in a family of *asuras*, his nature was not like theirs. He was steady and fearless in the face of danger and did not attach any importance to worldly affairs. He was not in the least attracted by selfish activities. He always controlled his senses and life force and possessed a perfectly steady intelligence and sense of discrimination. He was always happy and satisfied. All learned people praised him. In assemblies where there were discourses about saintly people, even his enemies would cite his character as an example of a great personality.[2] His glories were beyond description. He was a pure devotee of God.

In his childhood, Prahlad was always absorbed in meditation on God instead of playing like a normal child. He had no attraction for this world and preferred to remain deeply immersed in thoughts of God. Because he always served the Lord while sitting, traveling, eating, drinking, resting, sleeping, speaking, etc., he did not at all view any of these things from the platform of material enjoyment. Deeply immersed in love of Krishna, he would sometimes cry, sometimes laugh and sometimes sing and dance. He was overflowing with love and joy. Sometimes, while meditating on God in a state of deep concentration, he would enact the pastimes of the Lord. Sometimes he would even feel the touch of the Lord's hands. Then, after offering his obeisances with great pleasure, he would become silent with half-closed eyes full of tears of joy.

Prahlad had the good fortune to meet the great devotee sage Nārada Muni, who is completely detached from all material enjoyment. Due to this rare association Prahlad obtained pure devotion to the Supreme Lord, Who is known as Uttamaśloka (one who is praised with elevated poetry). Thus he always experienced the greatest pleasure in serving the Lord. After meeting holy Prahlad, even non-devotees and those unfortunate people who were leading irreligious lives began to feel some attraction for God, bringing them peace and happiness.

Now, Śrī Śukrācārya was the family priest of the Daityas. He had two sons named Ṣaṇḍa and Amarka, who lived near the palace of Hiraṇyakaśipu. At that time, as was the custom of their society, Hiraṇyakaśipu sent Prahlad to be educated at the school where the two sons of his guru Śukrācārya taught politics to the children of the *asuras*. Prahlad cleverly managed to maintain a good profile at school, listening to the teachers just as other students did, reading and repeating their lessons as requested. Yet in his mind he viewed the science of politics as nonsensical illusory knowledge and did not like it at all.

One day, upon returning to his home, his father took him very affectionately on his lap and inquired from him, "Dear child Prahlad, please tell me what is the best thing according to your understanding."

Hiraṇyakaśipu did not ask a specific question about Prahlad's school subjects, because he reasoned that the child might not know the answer from the textbooks and would feel embarrassed and ashamed. He preferred to ask a general question which the child could answer easily, according to his liking. Hiraṇyakaśipu hoped that Prahlad would tell him something about the subjects he was learning at school. Although Prahlad could understand his father's intentions very well, he considered that it was his duty to say something truthful, because he was in the presence of many people. Thus Prahlad spoke as follows:

"O best of the demons, I shall now tell you what is the best knowledge, according to my opinion. When an embodied living entity obtains temporary objects, his intelligence is inevitably disturbed. Living in the association of such persons is like staying in a dark well. Therefore, after leaving their house and going to the forest, one should take shelter of the lotus feet of Śrī Hari."

According to social custom, a child should always be respectful to his father, but here we see that Prahlad addressed his father as "greatest among the demons". *Asuras*, or demons, are never interested in discussing subjects that are good or auspicious, nor are they interested in the conversation of *sādhus*. So we can imagine how incredible it was for Hiraṇyakaśipu, the king of demons, to ask to hear something genuinely good from his son. Prahlad hinted at this, by addressing him as "O greatest *asura*", because such a great demon was asking about the most important and beneficial thing in life. We should try to understand and accept these four important instructions of Prahlad:

1. Temporary objects cannot give happiness
2. On the contrary, they give only misery and problems
3. One should give up a materialistic family in the same way that one escapes from a dry well
4. One should choose to live in a quiet place, taking shelter at the feet of Śrī Hari

An empty and dry well is a dark well, where no one goes to fetch water. If someone falls into such a dry well, he will not have any hope of escaping, as no one will come to rescue him. In the same way, if one lives in a house where there is no respect for *sādhus*, no one will come to rescue him from the hell of material life. One who wishes to obtain real benefit should leave a house that is never visited by *sādhus*.

Living in a quiet place does not imply that we should leave the city or village and go to live in the jungle. There is no such necessity, especially if one considers that the jungle itself would become a city if everyone went to live there. The meaning of this instruction is that we should live in a peaceful environment, leading a regulated *sattvik* life, following the principles of renunciation. This is the inner meaning of "going to live in the forest".

vanaṁ tu sāttviko vāso
grāmo rājasa ucyate
tāmasaṁ dyūta-sadanaṁ
man-niketaṁ tu nirguṇam
(Śrīmad Bhāgavatam, 11.25.25)

A sage, or *sādhu* is one who takes shelter of the lotus feet of Śrī Hari, Who is the complete Absolute Truth. There is no need of taking shelter of incomplete things. A saintly *sādhu* is a person who always takes shelter of Śrī Vishnu.

After hearing these words from the mouth of his son, Hiraṇyakaśipu laughed and said, "Someone has spoiled the intelligence of this ignorant child. He definitely must have heard these ideas from some Vaiṣṇava and is now repeating them." With this understanding, he gave orders to his demon servants: "O Daityas, take this child back to the house of his teachers and keep very strict guard over him, so that no *sādhu* will be able to come in contact with him, even if disguised. In fact, be very careful not to allow any *sādhu* to even enter my capital, lest he should spoil our children's understanding."

The demons took Prahlad back to the house of his teachers, and carefully reported the words that Hiraṇyakaśipu had spoken about Prahlad. Ṣaṇḍa and Amarka were very frightened and began to think, "If Prahlad goes to the king praising devotion to Vishnu, the king might think that we have taught it to him and he will punish us accordingly. This idea of worshiping Vishnu has not come from us, so he must have heard it from some Vaiṣṇava. Now we shall ask Prahlad in a shrewd way where he derived such knowledge. After obtaining this information we shall capture the culprit and bring him tied up before the king. In this way we shall amply demonstrate our loyalty to the king."

With this intention, they addressed Prahlad with very sweet words: "Dear Prahlad, all good fortune to you! Please tell us the truth, and do not lie to your teachers. We have instructed you together with the other boys of your class, yet no one else has obtained the knowledge that you now have. Rather, it is quite the opposite. Please tell us, from whom did you get this rare knowledge? O descendant of a great dynasty, did someone else convince you about this against our teachings or is this idea coming only from you? We are very interested to know this. Please do not keep any secrets from your teachers."

Prahlad answered, "Many times I had heard of people caught up in illusion and falling into the māyā of the Lord, making them see everything according to the false identifications of 'me' and 'them'. Today I have practically witnessed the demonstration of such illusion. I offer my respectful obeisances to the Supreme Lord, the master of this illusion. Only by the mercy of the Lord this misunderstanding, which divides the world into friends and enemies, will be cleared. If even Brahmā, Rudra, all the greatest demigods, ṛṣis and followers of the Vedas are subject to this energy of the Lord, then what can be said of those who think only in terms of friends and enemies? Know that it was God Himself Who shaped my understanding. O brāhmaṇas, just as iron is naturally attracted to a magnet, my heart is naturally attracted to Lord Vishnu."

Hearing Prahlad's intelligent reply, the two teachers became very frustrated because they could not obtain the answers they wanted. Actually they had hoped that Prahlad would tell them some particular name, so that they could catch that person and present him to the emperor to avoid becoming the target of his wrath. Now that their plan had failed they became very angry and began to scold Prahlad. They shouted, "Hurry, someone bring a stick! If we don't beat this disgrace of the family, he will not get the instruction he requires. This disgraceful boy has destroyed the name and fame of our family. Among the four kinds of actions—sama [being friendly], dana [offering gifts], bheda [dividing others], and daṇḍa [punishing]—he must definitely be punished as there is no other way of dealing with him. The dynasty of the Daityas is like a garden of sandalwood trees, but this child took birth in it as a thorny tree. Vishnu is like an axe to cut down and uproot the family of the Daityas, and this Prahlad is the strong wood which will supply the handle for the axe, so that the destruction can be completed."

The teachers of Prahlad were scolding him severely, but they did not have the courage to beat him because he was the son of the king. After some time they again began to teach Prahlad with great care and attention the principles of dharma, artha and kāma and three kinds of śāstras that could inspire him to follow this path. After a few days, they ascertained that Prahlad had learned everything about the science of politics (such as sama, dana, etc.), because he was able to answer all their questions properly. Feeling very happy, they first took the boy back to his mother.

The queen was extremely happy to see her child and bathed him very nicely, smearing his body with perfume and decorating him with auspicious marks. She then dressed him with beautiful clothes and many valuable ornaments. After this, the teachers took Prahlad to see King Hiraṇyakaśipu.

Prahlad offered his respects as soon as he arrived in the presence of his father. Seeing his son prostrated at his feet, Hiraṇyakaśipu blessed him and embraced him with both arms, taking great pleasure in this. He then took the child on his lap and, drenching him with tears of joy, said with a pleasant smile, "O Prahlad, my dear child, may you live long! Please tell me whatever good things you like best among the teachings you have learned from your gurus."

After being questioned in this way by his father, Prahlad thought, "These two sons of Śukrācārya are not bona fide teachers. The scriptures state that a sad-guru, a real guru, must have two qualities. The first is sutriya: he must know the scriptures very well. The second is brahma-niṣṭhā: he must have full faith in God. It can be said that Ṣaṇḍa and Amarka know the scriptures well, but they have no faith in God. On the contrary, they are very attached to material objects and therefore they cannot be considered to be real gurus. I have had the opportunity to learn viṣṇu-bhakti, devotion to Vishnu, from Nārada Muni, who is my real guru. I can say something from the teachings of Ṣaṇḍa and Amarka as my father desires, yet, because I have been asked in the presence of others, I shall speak about the instructions of my real sad-guru, Nārada Muni."

After reflecting upon this, Prahlad answered his father's question as follows: "The highest form of knowledge is the desire to surrender to Vishnu and to strive to please Him directly by means of the nine paths of devotion, such as listening to and reciting anything related to Vishnu [viṣṇu-kathā], remembering Him, serving His lotus feet, worshiping Him, offering Him respect, serving His instructions, becoming His friend and giving oneself to Him completely, with body, mind and speech. I consider that a person who regularly practices all this has learned the best science."

Herein, Prahlad explains that viṣṇu-bhakti, devotion to Vishnu, is the greatest of all knowledge. There are two kinds of knowledge—parā and aparā—transcendental knowledge and mundane knowledge, or spiritual and material.

dve vidye veditavye iti ha sma
yad brahma-vido vadanti parā caivāparā ca
parā yayā tad akṣaram adhigamyate
(Muṇḍaka Upaniṣad, 1.4-5)

Muṇḍaka Upaniṣad explains that parā-vidyā, superior knowledge (which is spiritual and transcendental) is that knowledge which allows us to understand the indestructible Brahman.

tat karma hari-toṣaṁ yat
sā vidyā tan-matir yayā
(Śrīmad Bhāgavatam, 4.29.49)

Śrīmad Bhāgavatam explains that vidyā is that knowledge with which we can please Hari, by remembering and meditating on Him. Such knowledge constitutes the sole duty of the living entity.

prabhu kahe—kon vidyā vidyā-madhye sāra?
rāya kahe—kṛṣṇa-bhakti vinā vidyā nāhi āra
(Śrī Caitanya Caritāmṛta, Madhya-līlā, 8.245)

Mahāprabhu said, "What is the essence of knowledge among all knowledge?" Rāmānanda Rāya said, "Without kṛṣṇa-bhakti there is no knowledge."

In this verse, Śrī Chaitanya Mahāprabhu explains the cream of all knowledge, citing the answer of Rāmānanda, "Knowledge of kṛṣṇa-bhakti is the best knowledge." Śrīla Bhaktisiddhanta Saraswati Ṭhākura explains, "Above knowledge that gives material enjoyment, there is brahma-vidyā, spiritual knowledge. Of spiritual knowledge, knowledge of devotion to Vishnu is superior and knowledge of devotion to Krishna is supreme." After describing the science of knowledge, Śrīla Bhaktisiddhanta Saraswati Ṭhākura continues: "Here, śravaṇa is described as hearing descriptions of the Name, Form, Qualities, Associates and Pastimes of Śrī Krishna. We must understand, step by step, that the same meaning applies also to kīrtana (reciting or singing) and smaraṇa (remembering). In particular, the meaning of smaraṇa is the contemplation of these topics within one's mind. Smaraṇa brings one to dhārana, which is the keeping of one's attention on things that are related to the Lord, which in turn becomes dhyāna, meditation, and finally samādhi, constant remembrance of the Lord. The meaning of pāda-sevana must be applied according to time and place, and concerns service such as taking darśana of the Deities, touching Them, respectfully circumambulating Them and following Them in procession. Visiting the temple of the Lord, the River Ganges and the holy places such as Puruṣottama-dhāma (Purī), Dvārakā-dhāma, Mathurā-dhāma, etc., and serving Tulasī and the Vaiṣṇavas are also considered to be forms of pāda-sevana bhakti. The meaning of arcana is the worship of Vishnu, the meaning of vandana is the offering of obeisances and prayers, and the meaning of dāsya is to always consider oneself to be the servant of the Lord. The meaning of sakhya is to cultivate a friendly attitude toward the Lord, always desiring the best for Him, thinking of Him and speaking of Him often. The meaning of ātmā-nivedana is to offer the Lord whatever we have, from our body to our pure soul and all else. Engagement in these nine ways of serving the Lord is considered to be bhakti, devotion. Furthermore, it is recommended to regularly practice these forms of service as gradual sādhana.

"Initially, we might do all this for our own benefit, but ultimately we should learn to perform this service only for the pleasure of Vishnu, always thinking this to be the real goal. The teachings of Prahlad are meant to show that the understanding or knowledge of a sādhaka, who practices devotion to the Lord in the above-mentioned ways, is the best kind of knowledge. The scriptures say that Śrī Parīkṣit Maharaj practiced service to the Lord by means of hearing hari-kathā (śravaṇa), Śrī Śukadeva by reciting it (kīrtana), Prahlad by remembering the Lord (smaraṇa), Śrī Lakṣmī Devī by serving His lotus feet (pāda-sevana), Pṛthu Maharaj by worshiping Him (arcana), Akrura by offering Him prayers and obeisances (vandana), Hanuman by executing His orders (dāsya), Arjuna by becoming His friend (sakhya) and Bāli Maharaj by offering everything to Him (ātmā-nivedana). By practicing only one out of these nine types of devotion, they each attained perfection in the service of the Lord."

Upon hearing from the lips of his own son Prahlad that serving and worshiping Vishnu is the best type of knowledge, Hiraṇyakaśipu felt sure that such ideas had been taught to Prahlad by his teachers. Out of terrible anger his lips started to tremble and he shouted insults at Ṣaṇḍa, the son of his guru: "O most unworthy brāhmaṇa! You idiot! What have you done? You have insulted me by taking the side of my enemy, teaching this ignorant child meaningless devotion to Vishnu!"

One may commit sinful activities in secret, but sooner or later such activities become manifest in the form of a disease or other symptoms. Similarly in this world there are many ill-natured people who dress like sādhus or act like friends, but their true nature will be manifested in time. King Hiraṇyakaśipu was blaming the sons of his family guru, and they were very anxious to avoid any blame, so they answered, "O conqueror of Indra, the three worlds tremble before your power and even the lord of Svarga is afraid of you. How could a lowly person like me gather the courage to take sides against you? Believe me, your son Prahlad said that these ideas are the result of his spontaneous and inborn nature and have not been learned from anyone else. Please do not get angry. Do not blame us."

At that time, in Satya Yuga, everyone was truthful, so there was no good reason to doubt the words of others. Hiraṇyakaśipu accepted the truthfulness of the words of the son of his guru and again inquired from his son Prahlad, "O disgrace and destruction of the family! If you did not get these ideas from the teachings of your gurus, then how could you become so unfaithful and disgraceful? How did your mind turn to this inauspicious path? Answer this question!"

Śrī Prahlad replied, "It is not possible to obtain devotion for Krishna from those who are attached to material life or from those who follow them. Those materialistic people (who follow gṛha-vrata) are fully engaged in enjoying their senses without restriction, so they fall into the darkest hell and go on chewing the already chewed. Although these two gurus, Ṣaṇḍa and Amarka, have knowledge of the Vedas, they are unable to understand that Vishnu is the only object of the Vedas. Because they are full of material desires, they remain attracted by the sweet words and flowery language of the karma-kāṇḍa [section of the Vedas dealing with fruitive activities]. Just as a blind man cannot show the right path to another blind man, they cannot teach me devotion to Vishnu because their eyes are densely covered by the three guṇas [material qualities]. Unless one purifies himself with the dust of the lotus feet of a mahātmā, who has no material desires, it is not possible to come in touch with the lotus feet of Lord Urukrama [one who performs great feats]. If one should be so fortunate as to encounter such a rare soul, then, by sincerely engaging his heart and soul in service of the feet of Śrī Krishna, all anarthas [bad qualities and habits] will disappear."

Prahlad explains herein that gṛha-vratis, those who are engrossed in a materialistic lifestyle, irrationally make their home the focal point of all their efforts and activities. They exhibit no faith in Krishna. One may raise the objection that a sādhu also stays inside a house, or gṛha. However, while externally a sādhu may indeed live in a house, internally he has no attachment to it. "Na gṛhaṁ gṛham ity āhur gṛhiṇī gṛham ucyate." Home, or gṛha, is not so much a place to live as it is the mentality of maintaining sense gratification, based upon wife and family as the center of all of a man's actions. Such a lusty man is called gṛha-vrati.

There are two other meanings of the expression gṛha-vrata. This body is made of the five gross elements and the subtle body, composed of mind, intelligence and ego. Therefore, in one sense, even the soul living inside these two bodies is living within a house. Those who are always engaged in the care, pampering and enjoyment of the body are called deha-sarvasva-vādi, and those who are dedicated to following whatever their mind dictates are called mano-dharmī. Both are called gṛha-vrati.

In these teachings Prahlad explains that knowledge and education that drive one toward excessive attachment to family life, lusty desire, identification with the body or uncontrolled mind, can only form a materialistic population of gṛha-vratis. Such people can never develop interest in Krishna's lotus feet, either by their own effort or by obtaining the help of others. Materialists do not care to control their senses. Therefore, their attachment to temporary things, bereft of real value, plunges them into the darkest depths of ignorance. To provide an example, we can again present the case of the two sons of Śukrācārya, who, in spite of studying the Vedas, could not understand kṛṣṇa-bhakti. Because of this, they cannot be considered to be actual followers of the Vedas. Truly, the only purpose of the Vedas is to teach viṣṇu-bhakti.

vedaiś ca sarvair aham eva vedyo
vedānta-kṛd veda-vid eva cāham
(Bhagavad-gītā, 15.15)

All the Vedas are meant to make us understand Śrī Krishna but, without the mercy of the Supreme Lord, no one can understand Him. Śrī Kaṭhopaniṣad says:

nāyam ātmā pravacanena labhyo
na medhayā na bahunā śrutena
yam evaiva vṛṇute tena labhyas
tasyaiva ātmā vivṛṇute tanūṁ svām
(Śrī Kaṭhopaniṣad, 2.23)

It is not possible to know the Lord either by lectures (pravacana), by intelligence (medha) or by learning. Only those who are surrendered to the Lord can come to know Him by His grace.

anumāna pramāṇa nahe iśvara-tattva-jñāne
kṛpā vinā iśvarere keha nāhi jāne
iśvarera kṛpā-leśa haya ta' yāhāre
sei ta' īśvara-tattva jānibāre pāre
(Śrī Caitanya Caritāmṛta, Madhya-līlā, 6.82-83)

It is not possible to obtain knowledge of God by means of speculation or proof. Without the mercy of God, no one can know Him. On the other hand, one who receives even a drop of mercy from the Lord will be able to obtain knowledge of Him.

The Lord manifests Himself directly and personally in the heart of a surrendered soul. Therefore, complete surrender and devotion to Vishnu is the main teaching of the Vedas. One may pose the question: if viṣṇu-bhakti is the only subject of the Vedas, why then do the Vedas talk about dharma, artha, kāma and fruitive activities? The answer to this is that the Vedas speak about these topics to attract those ignorant conditioned souls who are attached to material sense objects. It is said, "khanda laḍḍu kanyaya." Just as an immature child is shown some sweet laḍḍu to convince him to take an unpalatable medicine, the Vedas contain some sections that are very attractive to the ignorant. They encourage them by promoting fruitive activities in accordance with the Vedic path, so that they may ultimately become favorable toward following the Vedas and the Lord.

A parent or a doctor may offer some sweets to a sick child, but actually their intent is not to feed the child sweets, rather, to convince the child to take a medicine to cure his disease. In the same way, the karma-kāṇḍa section of the scriptures, which deals with fruitive activities, is not meant to increase attachment for karma in the conditioned souls, but rather, to lead them gradually toward the freedom of nirguṇa bhagavad-bhakti, devotion to the Lord unencumbered by material qualities and influences. Those who have very strong material desires cannot understand the actual and primary teaching of the Vedas. Therefore, they must be encouraged in some way.

Prahlad discusses how the conditioned soul can develop attraction for Krishna. Unless and until one gets the full blessing of a pure devotee, a mahat, it is impossible to come into contact with Krishna's lotus feet. A person who has no attachment to material things, without desire for that which is temporary and perishable, and who has love for and faith in Śrī Krishna, the Supreme Absolute Truth, the origin of everything, including Brahman, is called a mahat. Prahlad Maharaj says herein that he obtained devotion to Vishnu due to the mercy of a mahā-bhāgavata, Śrī Nārada, who was completely free from all material attachment. The two so-called family gurus, Ṣaṇḍa and

Amarka, could not transmit any devotion for Krishna by means of their teachings.

Seated upon his throne, Hiraṇyakaśipu resentfully listened to the speech of his little boy. Blinded by rage he threw Prahlad off his lap onto the ground, with the intention of killing him. How could he tolerate this boy threatening the family lineage? Seeing that Prahlad did not suffer any injury from his brutal act, Hiraṇyakaśipu began to shout with eyes reddened by anger, "Rākṣasas! Take this child away immediately and kill him without delay, because I want him dead."

Upon hearing this instruction, the Rākṣasas became confused. "What is the king saying? Who should we kill? This is his own son, Prahlad." Hiraṇyakaśipu saw their astonishment and loudly reiterated, "Why are you hesitating? This miserable wretch is not my son! Rather, he is a killer of my brother. Otherwise, how could he betray his own family by serving the feet of Vishnu, the slayer of my brother? How could he give up his parents and well-wishers while only five years old? This traitor could one day betray Vishnu as well. What is the guarantee that he will keep his faith? And how can he be sure that untrustworthy Vishnu will be true to his side?"

Even after receiving such clear orders, the Rākṣasas could not gather the courage to kill Prahlad. Hiraṇyakaśipu then proceeded to explain. "If some beneficial medicinal plant grows in the forest, we shall protect it carefully. In the same way, if the son of someone else is very favorable to us, we shall give him all protection and affection. On the other hand, we shall never protect a disease which has appeared in our own body and which can destroy it. Rather, we shall try to remove such an infection. In the same way, if our own son becomes hostile to us, he must be given up at once. If one's body is contaminated by infection and some limb starts to rot, it is necessary to cut off this limb and discard it in order to protect the rest of the body. Likewise, if we wish to protect the dynasty of the Daityas, the proper treatment is to remove this child. Just as the uncontrolled senses are the enemies of the yogi, this wicked Prahlad is my greatest enemy, even if he appears to be a friend and family member. Therefore you should kill him without a doubt. Do not hesitate in any way!"

Thus encouraged by King Hiraṇyakaśipu, all the Rākṣasas raised a frightening tumultuous sound. They shouted, "Kill him! Kill him!" while brandishing their spears. They cruelly tried to pierce the vital body parts of Prahlad, who was immersed in meditation on Śrī Hari and not paying them any attention. However, just as those who have no accumulated credit of pious activities fail in their plans, all the efforts of the demons were for naught. In the same way that the Supreme Lord cannot be described by words, being free from all material qualities, Prahlad could not be hurt by any weapon. Due to his complete absorption in meditation on Śrī Govinda, Prahlad sat on the lap of the Lord, thoroughly protected by Him from any attack. Though difficult to believe, such a thing is definitely possible. The Supreme Lord resides at the core of all things that exist, including demons and their weapons, controlling everything. Without His consent, no one can destroy anyone or protect anyone. Seeing that all the efforts of the Daityas were in vain, Hiraṇyakaśipu became afraid. He tied up Prahlad for the time being and contemplated different methods of killing him.

First of all, he tried to have Prahlad crushed by a herd of elephants. Then he tried to have him bitten by great poisonous snakes. Failing to accomplish his goal, he then tried to kill the boy by means of black magic, then by throwing him off the peak of a very high mountain, by burying him alive, by poisoning his food, by starving him, by freezing him with large quantities of ice, by blowing him away with a very powerful wind, by throwing him into fire, by submerging him in water and by hurling huge stones at him. Hiraṇyakaśipu tried in countless ways to harm Prahlad, but all his efforts failed.

After trying in so many ways to kill the innocent boy, the lord of the Daityas realized that he could not do any harm to Prahlad. He now became very anxious and started to think, "I have abused this boy with many harsh words and I have tried to kill him with different weapons. Yet he has such tremendous power that he cannot be harmed in any way. Even face-to-face with me, he remains fearless. Just as it is not possible to alter the inherent nature of a thing, such as straightening the curled tail of a dog, this boy will never rescind his misbehavior toward me. He will always be hostile to me and he will also never forget Vishnu. This boy possesses a great unconquerable power, remaining fearless under all circumstances. He must be immortal. If I fight against him, I might even die myself."

The lord of the demons could see that his own power was diminishing and, as a result, he became overwhelmed by anxiety and despondency. Then the two sons of Śukrācārya, Ṣaṇḍa and Amarka, approached him in a solitary place and tried to pacify him.

"O lord, all kings become frightened by the mere threat of the movement of your eyes. Single-handedly you have conquered all the three worlds. Why are you feeling such anxiety? Little children do not know what is good and what is bad; they are ignorant and foolish. Therefore, there is no merit or fault in their activities. Let Śukrācārya now come back so that we may ask him for his advice. In the meantime, scare Prahlad and do not allow him any chance to escape. Bind him with the magical ropes of Varuṇa. In this way, he will not be exposed to contact with sādhus and perhaps with time, when he has grown up, he will change his mind."

Hiraṇyakaśipu accepted this advice and replied, "Yes, we shall do this. You will teach Prahlad the duties of a family man and king, and also about charity."

With great care, Ṣaṇḍa and Amarka again taught Prahlad about material religiosity, economic development and sense gratification. And again the boy studied his lessons and behaved very politely, but did not take their instructions very seriously. In fact, he never accepted their instructions as worthy, because all his teachers were attached to the material world and were therefore controlled by the dualities of attachment (rāga) and disgust (dveṣa).

One day, the teachers went to their homes to do some work, allowing the boys, who were now alone, the opportunity to amuse themselves by playing. The schoolmates of Prahlad called him to play with them. Yet Prahlad, who was very wise, smiled and replied with great affection, "Dear friends, please tell me what is the purpose of this world."

Those innocent boys still had pure hearts, uncontaminated by their contact with materialists who are attached to pleasure and pain. Because they loved Prahlad and respected him very much, they stopped playing and flocked around him. Sitting in a circle, they listened very attentively to his words. Prahlad then began to instruct his schoolmates.

kaumāra ācaret prājño
dharmān bhāgavatān iha
durlabhaṁ manuṣaṁ janma
tad apy adhruvam arthadam
(Śrīmad Bhāgavatam, 7.6.1)

"Those who are intelligent will engage in the service of the Lord (bhagavata-dharma) from an early age, because it is very rare to obtain a human life. A human birth is temporary, but extremely valuable."

Prahlad advises us to start devotional service to Śrī Hari in early childhood. One may ask how it is possible for small children, especially those who are born into demoniac families and have not been purified by the processes of initiation (saṁskāra, upanayana and dīkṣā), to actually observe this dharma. The answer to this question is that initiation is required only to facilitate the following of the varṇāśrama system, not to facilitate the following of the path of devotional service to the Supreme Lord, which is based upon hearing and chanting. All human beings are qualified to engage in bhagavata-dharma—devotional service to the Lord. However, we shouldn't think that devotional service is lower than varṇāśrama-dharma because no special qualifications are required to engage in devotional service, whereas varṇāśrama-dharma does require special qualifications. Actually, devotional service to the Lord is universal, and thus it is greater and more elevated than varṇāśrama-dharma. As the ocean is greater and deeper than any other water reservoir, so bhagavata-dharma is higher and deeper than any other thing. Śrī Vyāsadeva has said:

sa vai puṁsāṁ paro dharmo
yato bhaktir adhokṣaje
ahaituky apratihatā
yayātmā su-prasīdati
(Śrīmad Bhāgavatam, 1.2.6)

"Devotion to Lord Adhokṣaja constitutes the greatest dharma. Therefore, it is causeless and cannot be hampered by anything. Through this causeless devotion, the soul can obtain the greatest satisfaction."

"Adhokṣaja" means "That which is beyond the senses" and indicates Śrī Krishna.

etāvān eva loke 'smin
puṁsāṁ dharmaḥ paraḥ smṛtaḥ
bhakti-yogo bhagavati
tan-nāma-grahaṇādibhiḥ
(Śrīmad Bhāgavatam, 6.3.22)

Bhakti-yoga, devotional service to the Lord, which begins by hearing and reciting His Name, is the greatest dharma (duty or religion) for the soul. The compiler of the Vedas, Śrī Krishna Dvaipāyana Vyāsadeva, compiled Śrīmad Bhāgavatam after compiling the Vedas and their divisions, the Vedanta and all the Purāṇas. Following the instructions of his spiritual master, Śrī Nārada Muni, he composed the four original verses of Śrīmad Bhāgavatam and then expanded them into 18,000 to explain the supreme duty or religion for all mankind, which has no equal or superior and which is opposed to hypocritical material religiosity. This work gave him full spiritual satisfaction.

Again, one might object that these demon boys were only boys, and that at their age one is not expected to engage in religiosity but rather in playing and sports. Devotional service can be more properly executed later on in life, in adolescence, adulthood or old age, but we must admit that no one is guaranteed to live long enough to reach adolescence, adulthood or old age. Those who are truly intelligent will begin devotional service to Śrī Hari as soon as possible. One might again object that, if we cannot serve the Lord in this lifetime, we will do so in our next one, but the reply to this is that a human birth is extremely rare. If, by extreme good fortune, we have obtained this human form of life, we should not consider it as permanent or eternal, because at any time we can lose this unique opportunity. Today I am alive, but there is no guarantee that I will still be alive tomorrow. The great value of human life is that even in a moment it is possible to attain success in devotional service. Therefore, every single moment of a human life is extremely valuable.

In the Puranas, it is said that Maharaj Khatvanga, after surrendering to the lotus feet of Śrī Vishnu, attained perfection in a single moment. What was possible for him is also possible for others. In the śāstras, those who waste the very valuable time of their human lives are called ātmā-hatyas, indicating that they are committing suicide.

nṛ-deham ādyaṁ sulabhaṁ sudurlabhaṁ
plavaṁ su-kalpaṁ guru-karṇadhāram
mayānukūlena nabhasvateritaṁ
pumān bhavābdhiṁ na taret sa ātma hā
(Śrīmad Bhāgavatam, 11.20.17)

Prahlad continued:

yathā hi puruṣasyeha
viṣṇoḥ pādopasarpaṇam
yad eṣa sarva-bhūtānāṁ
priya ātmeśvaraḥ suhṛt
(Śrīmad Bhāgavatam, 7.6.2)

"Coming in touch with the lotus feet of Vishnu means serving the lotus feet of the Supreme Lord, which is the highest duty for all human beings. Śrī Vishnu is the supreme object of love, the supreme controller, the well-wisher and soul of all living entities."

To approach the lotus feet of Śrī Vishnu is to execute the process of devotional service in four basic sentiments: śānta-rati (neutral attachment), dāsya-bhāva (servitorship), sakhya-bhāva (friendship) and kānta-bhāva (conjugal love). The following of any one of these methods is known as bhagavata-dharma, devotional service to the Lord.

One of the meanings of ātmā is "son". The implication is that there is such a thing as devotional service in vātsalya-rasa (parenthood). Therefore, all the five main rasas are included in the worship of Śrī Krishna: śānta, dāsya, sakhya, vātsalya and mādhurya.

sukham aindriyakaṁ daityā
deha-yogena dehinām
sarvatra labhyate daivād
yathā duḥkham ayatnataḥ
(Śrīmad Bhāgavatam, 7.6.3)

"O children of the Daityas, the pleasure of sense gratification is available in all life forms, even in the bodies of animals and birds. Just as we receive suffering even without searching for it, sense gratification will come according to our previous karma [activities]. Therefore, after obtaining this valuable human life, you do not need to strive for sense enjoyment because, by this unnecessary effort, valuable time is wasted."

tat-prayāso na kartavyo
yata āyur-vyayaḥ param
na tathā vindate kṣemaṁ
mukunda-caraṇāmbujam
(Śrīmad Bhāgavatam, 7.6.4)

"By engaging in the devotional service of the lotus feet of Lord Mukunda, we shall obtain benefits that are far greater than those which can be obtained through material enjoyment. Lord Mukunda will grant us liberation from the bondage of material life. He will give the real pleasure of life. No other worshipable personality is able to rescue us from the clutches of birth and death."

In Bhagavad-gītā, Śrī Krishna says:

ā-brahma-bhuvanāl lokāḥ
punar āvartino 'rjuna
mām upetya tu kaunteya
punar janma na vidyate
(Bhagavad-gītā, 8.16)

"O Arjuna, in this universe all planets, including Brahmāloka, are temporary places from which one must fall down, while those who attain Me will not have to take another birth."

The Purāṇas narrate the episode of a great war between the devas (demigods) and the asuras. In this war Maharaj Khatvaṅga formed an alliance with the devas and defeated the demons. The demigods were very pleased with him and wanted to offer him a boon, so King Khatvaṅga prayed for deliverance from death. The devas told him that no one can give protection from death, except for the Supreme Lord, Vishnu. Immediately, the king left the company of the demigods and fully surrendered to Śrī Vishnu.

tato yateta kuśalaḥ
kṣemāya bhavam āśritaḥ
śarīraṁ pauruṣaṁ yāvan
na vipadyeta puṣkalam
(Śrīmad Bhāgavatam, 7.6.5)

"For this reason, one who is intelligent will fear the sufferings of material existence, and understand that without devotional service to the Lord one will fall from his position (na bhajanti avajananti sthanad bhrastaḥ padanti adaḥ). In other words, without serving the Lord there can be no relief from misery.

Having properly understood this point, one should sincerely pursue the real benefit of human life by engaging in devotional service to the Lord in early childhood, before being attacked by disease and old age."

When old age makes one an invalid, it becomes very difficult to engage in devotional service because of physical weakness and attachment to the material senses and mind. Therefore, one who is intelligent, with a vision of the future, will think ahead, realizing what results the future may bring. Such a person will be very careful about their spiritual life even from childhood.

puṁso varṣa-śataṁ hy āyus
tad-ardhaṁ cājitātmanaḥ
niṣphalaṁ yad asau rātryāṁ
śete 'ndhaṁ prāpitas tamaḥ

mugdhasya bālye kaiśore
krīḍato yāti viṁśatiḥ
jarayā grasta-dehasya
yāty akalpasya viṁśatiḥ

durāpūreṇa kāmena
mohena ca balīyasā
śeṣaṁ gṛheṣu saktasya
pramattasyāpayāti hi
(Śrīmad Bhāgavatam, 7.6.6-8)

"A human life lasts approximately one hundred years and, during this short span of life, those who are controlled by their senses can only take advantage of fifty of these years, as they invariably spend their nights covered by ignorance and deep sleep. Of the remaining time, ten years are spent with no facility for understanding during childhood, another ten years in playing and sporting during adolescence and, during old age, the last twenty years of one's life are spent as an invalid in a life of retirement. The remaining time (only twenty to thirty years) is usually spent in the pursuit of sense enjoyment and the formation of strong attachments that generate innumerable sufferings, resulting in the loss of one's very self in the deep illusion of bondage to home and family. There is no time left to search for one's real benefit."

ko gṛheṣu pumān saktam
ātmānam ajitendriyaḥ
sneha-pāśair dṛḍhair baddham
utsaheta vimocitum
(Śrīmad Bhāgavatam, 7.6.9)

"Gṛha indicates house, wife, children and family life. After having tied himself very tightly with the bondage of attachment and affection for children and family, what conditioned soul will be able to escape such bondage? Some people understand that they should engage in the service of Krishna but, due to attachment to family and relatives, their knowledge is spoiled by the illusion of material life and therefore they are unable to worship the Lord. Thus it is much better to start serving the Lord in early childhood, before attachment to material life has the opportunity to steal away the mind."

ko nv artha-tṛṣṇāṁ visṛjet
prāṇebhyo 'pi ya īpsitaḥ
yaṁ krīṇāty asubhiḥ preṣṭhais
taskaraḥ sevako vaṇik
(Śrīmad Bhāgavatam, 7.6.10)

"After developing attachment for money, who can give up the desire to acquire wealth and instead dedicate himself solely to the service of the Lord? Money must be dearer than life, because thieves, servants and businessmen are even prepared to sell their own souls and risk their lives in order to earn some wealth. Who can give up the desire for money?"

Attachment to money is an intense form of illusion that drives us to accumulate more and more wealth. When such a devouring desire becomes fixed in one's heart, there is no more time for service to the Lord.

kathaṁ priyāyā anukampitāyāḥ
saṅgaṁ rahasyaṁ rucirāṁś ca mantrān
suhṛtsu tat-sneha-sitaḥ śiśūnāṁ
kalākṣarāṇām anurakta-cittaḥ

putrān smaraṁs tā duhitṝr hṛdayyā
bhrātṝn svasṝr va pitarau ca dīnau
gṛhān manojñoru-paricchadāṁś ca
vṛttīś ca kulyāḥ paśu-bhṛtya-vargān

tyajeta kośas-kṛd ivehamānaḥ
karmāṇi lobhād avitṛpta-kāmaḥ
aupasthya-jaihvaṁ bahu-manyamānaḥ
kathaṁ virajyeta duranta-mohaḥ
(Śrīmad Bhāgavatam, 7.6.11-13)

Here, Prahlad very elaborately describes to his schoolmates the different kinds of attachments, explaining that it is necessary to start devotional service to Śrī Hari, even while still a child. He says, "You see, if you do not engage in devotional service from this point, when you grow up you will forget everything about God, due to association with your beloved wives. How will you be able to meditate on the Lord if you are always remembering the sweet words and requests of your wives? In addition to this, you will eventually beget children. Their awkward, cute words, spoken in broken language, will capture your ears and your heart. After developing such a strong attachment for your child, how will you be able to concentrate your mind on Śrī Hari? Besides the natural affection for a son, there will always be anxiety for a daughter who goes to live in the house of her in-laws, and you will be wondering when she will come to visit you and who will accompany her. Similarly, there will be affection for brothers and sisters and a feeling of duty and compassion toward your elderly parents. Dutiful sons always wonder, 'My poor father and mother are now invalids. If I do not take care of them, who will?' You will even be attached to clothes and other objects of pleasure for the family and all this will hinder your devotional service to the Lord.

"Besides all this, a child reared in a family of asuras will find it difficult to engage in the worship of Vishnu, due to the fact that according to their family tradition asuras are always hostile to Vishnu. We may also think that, since no one in our family has worshiped Vishnu, we should also not do so. Affection and attachment for servants and household animals will also occupy our minds and we will think, 'All these people have been working for me and I have always taken care of their families. Who will take care of them if I engage in other activities?' Who will be able to give up all these attachments and illusions and concentrate on the service of the Lord? Therefore those who are intelligent will begin service to Śrī Hari in early childhood.

"Just as a silkworm builds its cocoon with great care to enjoy its nice house, but leaves no exit and therefore dies in the process, those people who settle into family life in order to obtain sensual enjoyment, thinking mostly how to satisfy their own senses, such as belly, genitals, tongue etc., do not leave any way out of their entanglement [wife, sons, daughters, grandchildren, etc.] and become completely bound by material life. At the end, their house becomes their death, the cause of great misery. 'I built this house to become happy, but now this household life is burning like fire, reducing me to ashes.' How can one attain renunciation after entering this material life, since the illusion of material life is so difficult to overcome?"

kuṭumba-poṣāya viyan nijāyur
na budhyate 'rthaṁ vihataṁ pramattaḥ
sarvatra tāpa-traya-duḥkhitātmā
nirvidyate na sva-kuṭumba-rāmaḥ
(Śrīmad Bhāgavatam, 7.6.14)

"One whose heart is very deeply attached to family and relatives forgets all other thoughts and becomes lost in the act of taking care of them, wasting the valuable time of this very rare human life, which can be utilized to stop suffering, once and for all, and to attain permanent happiness. After getting this permanent benefit, everything is obtained. By knowing this, everything is known and nothing else remains to be attained or searched out, because by means of this human life one can attain the Supreme and Absolute Whole, God Himself. If one does not understand this, he is wasting his life away. People are very worried about wasting even a penny, but they will carelessly waste their entire life. One who is completely under the spell of illusion, due to attachment to family, will constantly burn in the fire of the threefold sufferings [those caused by one's body and mind, those caused by other living entities and those caused by nature], but they will never think for even one moment that material life is undesirable."

vitteṣu nityābhiniviṣṭa-cetā
vidvāṁś ca doṣaṁ para-vitta-hartuḥ
pretyeha vāthāpy ajitendriyas tad
aśānta-kāmo harate kuṭumbī
(Śrīmad Bhāgavatam, 7.6.15)

"Those who are always intensely concentrating their minds on property and family, and who are controlled by their senses, will never be satisfied with what they get. They will even steal, cheat and take away the property of others in order to get more and more money to maintain their own family. They will do this even though they know that such crimes will be punished by the king and will bring ill-repute and even punishment in the after-life at the hands of Yamarāja."

Attachment to the maintenance of one's family and the greed to acquire more and more wealth can drive people to commit all kinds of sinful acts and crimes. Prahlad lived in Satya Yuga, and from his explanation we can see that such things happen in any time period. In Kali Yuga, however, attachment for family and greed for wealth have spread like wildfire and have become the most important goals of life, influencing all the classes of society everywhere. Thus, due to the unrestrained desire to make money at any cost, the world has become a very dangerous place indeed.

vidvān apītthaṁ danujāḥ kuṭumbaṁ
puṣṇan sva-lokāya na kalpate vai
yaḥ svīya-pārakya-vibhinna-bhāvas
tamaḥ prapadyeta yathā vimūḍhaḥ
(Srimad Bhagavatam, 7.6.16)

"O young Dānavas, even intelligent persons become bound by excessive attachment to family and home, thinking, 'This is mine, this is not mine.' They build their lives based upon this kind of understanding, and their knowledge becomes covered by foolishness, forgetting the real welfare and true duty of the soul."

This understanding of reality based upon duality is a prime characteristic of the demons. From this kind of demoniac vision, all bad qualities and problems arise and one starts to behave improperly, with no respect for the regulations of the scriptures. Such persons take care of those people considered to be kith and kin, based solely upon bodily considerations. Without any remorse, they are quick to exploit and inflict suffering upon all others.

The sādhu, the saintly devotee, sees everyone as equal. He sees everyone as related to God and is therefore equally friendly to all living entities. Although he may see them according to their different capacities and behavior, he loves them all in the same way.

yato na kaścit kva ca kutracid vā
dīnaḥ svam ātmānam alaṁ samarthaḥ
vimocituṁ kāma-dṛśaṁ vihāra-
krīḍā-mṛgo yan-nigaḍo visargaḥ

tato vidūrāt parihṛtya daityā
daityeṣu saṅgaṁ viṣayātmakeṣu
upeta nārāyaṇam ādi-devaṁ
sa mukta-saṅgair iṣito 'pavargaḥ
(Śrīmad Bhāgavatam, 7.6.17-18)

"O sons of the Daityas, no matter where he lives or how learned in the scriptures he may be, a man who is hostile to the Lord and attached to his own family will not be able to free himself from material life. Such an unfortunate man is always thinking about enjoying sex with his wife. Surrounded by children and grand children, he becomes bound by illusion and blinded by deep attachment. Therefore I request you, please give up the association of those demons who are deeply attached to material enjoyment and take shelter of those liberated persons who have no material attachment and worship the lotus feet of the Supreme Lord, Śrī Nārāyaṇa."

na hy acyutaṁ prīṇayato
bahv-āyāso 'surātmajāḥ
ātmavāt sarva-bhūtānāṁ
siddhatvād iha sarvataḥ
(Śrīmad Bhāgavatam, 7.6.19)

"O children of the asuras! To please Lord Acyuta is easy, because He is always very near to us all. Contrarily, even after much effort and suffering it is impossible to please those we consider to be our family based upon bodily identification." Śrī Hari dwells in the heart of every living entity and to find Him is not difficult at all. In order to engage in His service, we do not require many material things as He can also be served within our minds.

A brāhmaṇa who lived in Pratisthapur attained Nārāyaṇa by means of mental worship, simply by saying, "O Lord, Śrī Hari, protector of my life, may You be pleased." Just by saying these words sincerely, he was able to please the Lord. In the worship of the Lord there is no consideration of age. Any surrendered soul, in childhood or old age, can please Him by hearing about and reciting His Name, Forms, Pastimes, etc.

tasmāt sarveṣu bhūteṣu
dayāṁ kuruta sauhṛdam
bhāvam āsuram unmucya
yayā tuṣyaty adhokṣajaḥ
(Śrīmad Bhāgavatam, 7.6.24)

"Therefore, my dear young Daityas, you should renounce all hatred and become kind and merciful to all living entities, considering yourselves to be the friends of everyone. If one is a devotee of the Lord and has developed love for Him, he will naturally show affection to all living entities. Please give up the mentality of the demons, who see everyone and everything from the perspective of duality. Instead, become affectionate to all living entities, knowing that they are all parts of the marginal potency of the Lord. Then Lord Adhokṣaja will be pleased. By the mercy of the guru and the Vaiṣṇavas, you will obtain devotion to the Lord and equal vision toward all entities."

God is the original cause of all causes, and if He is pleased there is nothing impossible to obtain. Surrendering unconditionally to the Supreme Lord is therefore the actual duty and welfare of the soul. Prahlad stresses this point, explaining to his schoolmates that the teachings he is offering to them do not represent his personal opinions, but a rare and pure knowledge he had learned from Nārada. Someone might ask how this small boy born in a family of asuras could ever have been able to hear from Nārada. In reply, we would say that good and qualified persons are not the only people eligible to hear the glories of the Lord. Anyone who comes into contact with the dust of the lotus feet of the pure devotees and obtains their blessings will also receive this pure knowledge.

śrutam etan mayā pūrvaṁ
jñānaṁ vijñāna-saṁyutam
dharmaṁ bhāgavataṁ śuddhaṁ
nāradād deva-darśanāt
(Śrīmad Bhāgavatam, 7.6.28)

"Previously, I heard this knowledge of devotional service to the Lord from Nārada Muni, who is a great soul and devotee."

The demon boys were amazed to hear that Prahlad was a student of Nārada, and asked:

"O Prahlad, we are always together and we have no other teachers except Ṣaṇḍa and Amarka. We do not know any other guru; only these two are our teachers and guides. We always live within the palace compound, so it is not easy for us to see or meet a great personality. How, then, can we believe that you have met the great sage Nārada and learned this knowledge from him? Please dispel our confusion."

Prahlad answered, "Our powerful father, Hiraṇyakaśipu, went to Mandara Mountain to engage in penance, so Indra and the other demigods hurriedly readied themselves for fighting and defeating the demons. Soon they attacked the kingdom and started to kill the Daityas, who fled in fear for their lives, leaving behind wives, children, household animals and houses. The triumphant demigods proceeded to seize all the properties of my father and destroy his residential palace. My mother Kayādhu was kidnapped by Indra, the king of the demigods, and started to cry piteously like a kurarī bird. At that time, Devārṣi Nārada took note of Indra's actions and stopped him. Indra, king of the devas, explained to Nārada that he did not have any bad intentions toward the queen but, since she was the wife of the great demon and was carrying his child in her womb, the demigods feared that, when the child grew up, he might become a tremendous problem like his father. So, he explained that as soon as the queen gave birth to the child, they would kill the infant and release the mother.

"Nārada told Indra, 'Do not follow this plan. The child inside the womb of this Daitya queen is a great devotee, a servant of

Ananta, and he cannot be killed.' After hearing that the unborn child was a devotee of Vishnu, Indra immediately released my mother and, after circumambulating her out of respect for her unborn child, he went back to the heavenly realm. My mother, however, was still in a desperate position, so Nārada Muni took pity on her and allowed her to stay in his āśrama until her husband returned.

"My mother served Nārada Muni with great care and Nārada, being very pleased by her service, offered her a boon. My mother thought, 'If I give birth in the āśrama of the ṛṣi, the āśrama will be polluted. Besides, my husband is far away, engaged in tapasya, and if I give birth to my son in his absence, I will endanger his life and find myself in a difficult position. Therefore I will ask a special boon: to be able to give birth to my child at any time I choose.' Nārada Muni agreed, desiring to offer her another boon. My mother was not able to follow the valuable instructions of Nārada, so she asked him if he could store all of his teachings in the mind of her unborn child. Nārada Muni accepted her prayer and granted that boon as well. So, while I was still living inside my mother's womb, I received the knowledge that enables one to distinguish between spirit and matter.

"A long time passed, and my mother forgot all the instructions she had heard from Nārada Muni, but now I have explained them to you. If you have faith in my words, you will obtain the knowledge of spirit and matter, just like anyone else who listens to them faithfully."

tatropāya-sahasrāṇām
ayaṁ bhagavatoditaḥ
yad iśvare bhagavati
yathā yair añjasā ratiḥ

guru-śuśrūṣayā bhaktyā
sarva-labdhārpaṇena ca
saṅgena sādhu-bhaktānām
īśvarārādhanena ca

śraddhayā tat-kathāyāṁ ca
kīrtanair guṇa-karmaṇām
tat-pādāmburuha-dhyānāt
tal-liṅgekṣārhaṇādibhiḥ
(Śrīmad Bhāgavatam, 7.7.29-31)

"The best form of devotion among thousands of practices, which directly bestows love of Godhead, is to serve the guru without the desire for anything in return. On the external platform, this pure devotion will destroy the seed of material existence. One should hear logical explanations from the guru, accept the caraṇāmṛta of the guru [the water which washed his lotus feet] on one's head and offer him everything one possesses, without consideration of name and fame. Furthermore, one should associate with good devotees, and engage in the worship of the Lord within one's mind or by the utilization of physical objects."

Viśvanātha Cakravartī Ṭhākura explains: "durācāro bhaktaḥ sevyaḥ vandyo darśanīyaś ca, na tu saṅgārtham upadeyaḥ." First of all, one should develop an interest in listening to the descriptions of the Lord and His beloved devotees, His Names, Qualities, Pastimes etc. It is said, "bhāgavata-kathā-śravaṇa-ruci-mūlā śraddhā." By listening to topics pertaining to the Lord with interest and faith, one will start to speak about, meditate on and remember the Lord's lotus feet. One will worship Him by going to the temple and so on, thus engaging in the path of devotion.

rāyaḥ kalatraṁ paśavaḥ sutādayo
gṛhā mahī kuñjara-kośa-bhūtayaḥ
sarve 'rtha-kāmāḥ kṣaṇa-bhaṅgurāyuṣaḥ
kurvanti martyasya kiyat priyaṁ calāḥ
(Śrīmad Bhāgavatam, 7.7.39)

"One who desires to engage in the enjoyment of the material objects of the senses will not find permanent pleasure. The greed to enjoy wealth, parents, wife, sons and other family members, household animals (such as elephants, cows and horses), house, land, treasury, opulence and money, etc., will use up all the time of human life, which is very short. Being temporary, such pleasures will not give true happiness. In other words, the soul cannot find happiness in matter."

sukhāya duḥkha-mokṣāya
saṅkalpa iha karmiṇaḥ
sadāpnotīhayā duḥkham
anīhāyāḥ sukhāvṛtaḥ
(Śrīmad Bhāgavatam, 7.7.42)

"In this world, all materialists try to obtain pleasure and avoid suffering, but they are happy only so long as they make plans for their future pleasure. When they actually try to get pleasure, they begin to suffer."

daiteyā yakṣa-rakṣāṁsi
striyaḥ śūdrā vrajaukasaḥ
khagā mṛgāḥ pāpa-jīvāḥ
santi hy acyutatāṁ gatāḥ
(Śrīmad Bhāgavatam, 7.7.54)

"On the path of devotion to the Lord, there are no distinctions based upon caste or race. Yakṣas, Rākṣasas, women, śūdras, cowherds and even sinners, animals and birds are eligible to taste the nectar of devotion to Lord Acyuta."

etāvān eva loke 'smin
puṁsaḥ svārthaḥ paraḥ smṛtaḥ
ekānta-bhaktir govinde
yat sarvatra tad-īkṣaṇam
(Śrīmad Bhāgavatam, 7.7.55)

The pure devotees of Govinda can see God present in all living entities, either residing on the land or in the water—nārāyaṇam ayaṁ dhīraḥ paśyanti paramārthinaḥ jagad dhanamayaṁ lubdhāḥ kāmukāḥ kāminīmayam. Prahlad could see God directly and personally present inside a pillar. This is the supreme goal, recommended by all the scriptures for all the human beings of this world.

The sons of the Daityas accepted the instructions of Prahlad and appreciated them very much, thereby rejecting the teachings of their demoniac gurus Ñaëòa and Amarka. Due to their association with Prahlad, the young Daityas became firmly resolved in their faith in Vishnu. Ñaëòa and Amarka, frightened by this turn of events, hurried to King Hiraëyakaçipu to explain what had happened.

Hearing the bad news, Hiraṇyakaśipu became overcome by a terrible rage and, with his body trembling from head to toe, decided to kill Prahlad personally. Hissing like a trampled snake, Hiraṇyakaśipu thundered insults at Prahlad, shouting that the boy was not even qualified to address him. With a very humble attitude and folded hands, Prahlad stood in front of Hiraṇyakaśipu, while the king, with a fierce stare, hurled cruel words at him:

"You arrogant, foolish boy, destroyer of the family! O miserable wretch, how dare you disrespect my commands! You idiot! I will send you to the abode of Yama, the lord of death, right now! O dull-headed child, all the kings of the world start to tremble when they see me angry. From where are you getting this power of remaining fearless before me?"

Prahlad answered:

na kevalaṁ me bhavataś ca rājan
sa vai balaṁ balināṁ cāpareṣām
pare 'vare 'mī sthira-jaṅgamā ye
brahmādayo yena vaśaṁ praṇītāḥ
(Śrīmad Bhāgavatam, 7.8.7)

"O King, this power of which you speak is not only my power but yours as well. It is the same power that sustains all living entities living on the land and in the water, high and low, starting from Brahmā and including all the creatures under his control. He is the only Supreme Controller, as well as Eternal Time and Death. He is the power of the senses and the power of the mind, the power of the body and the soul of all the senses, the Lord of the three guṇas [the qualities of material nature], unlimited and capable of conquering anyone. This Supreme Lord is the creator and destroyer of this world. Please give up your demoniac nature and dualistic vision based upon the concept of friends and enemies! You should see everyone equally, because our great and only enemy is our uncontrolled mind. Besides this enemy, there are no other enemies. Those who see everyone with equal vision are the best among the worshipers of the Lord.

"In the past, foolish people like yourself were also harassed by that same enemy, the uncontrolled mind. Lust, anger, illusion, greed, madness and envy are thieves who steal away everything from the unfortunate soul. Without conquering them, how can we think we have conquered the world? A sādhu who possesses equal vision and a controlled mind cannot have any enemy. Seeing enemies is only due to ignorance."

Enraged by the speech of Prahlad, Hiraṇyakaśipu shouted, "You idiot! How dare you oppose and insult me! Are you offending me, thinking that you have conquered all your enemies? I can definitely see that your death has come because, at the time of death, people lose their minds and start talking deliriously without making any sense. O miserable, wretched boy, who is lord in this world except me? If there is any Lord, where is He?"

Prahlad replied, "He is present everywhere."

Then Hiraṇyakaśipu asked, "If so, why do I not I see Him in this pillar?"

Prahlad said, "I see Him in this pillar."

Hiraṇyakaśipu thundered, "Ah, so He is in this pillar? I shall immediately cut your arrogant head off. Let your protector Hari come and save you!"

The powerful Hiraṇyakaśipu, blinded by rage, screamed and shouted while brandishing his curved sword and, springing up from his throne, he violently struck the pillar. A deafening sound came from within the pillar. Brahmā and all the demigods thought that the shell of the universe was cracking and feared that their planets might collapse. The leader of all the demons, Hiraṇyakaśipu, who was feared by all the kings of the demons, intended to kill his own son Prahlad; yet now he was taken aback by this terrible sound. Even after searching carefully he could not ascertain what the origin of it was.

satyaṁ vidhātuṁ nija-bhṛtya-bhāṣitaṁ
vyāptiṁ ca bhūteṣv akhileṣu cātmanaḥ
adṛśyatātyadbhuta-rūpam udvaham
stambhe sabhāyāṁ na mṛgaṁ na mānuṣam
(Śrīmad Bhāgavatam, 7.8.17)

Lord Śrī Hari heard the words of His own servant, Prahlad. Since He is present everywhere, He appeared in the pillar in His very wonderful form of Nṛsiṁha to support the truth of His devotee's statement. This frightening form, neither animal nor human, immediately began to kill all the demons. The Lord did not wish to compromise the words of Brahmā, also a servant of the Lord, who had promised that Hiraṇyakaśipu would not be killed by any human being or animal or by any other creature made by him, not indoors or outdoors, or by any weapon. The Lord also wanted to keep His own promise, "na me bhaktaḥ pranaśyati", as well as support the truth of Nārada Muni's words, who had said that Prahlad was a devotee of Ananta and therefore could not be killed. For all these reasons, Lord Nṛsiṁha appeared.

Although He appeared from within the pillar, God is not any sort of creature. Hiraṇyakaśipu saw this very wonderful form, but he could not see God. For him, this was not God, but a fantastic type of living entity, half man (nṛ) and half lion (siṁha). To see something in its true light, one has to possess the necessary qualities. Otherwise, one will not be able to see, even if that object is right in front of one's eyes. The Lord is fully perfect in Himself and is self-manifested. Just as it is possible to see the sun only through the power of the sun itself, seeing God is possible only by His mercy and not otherwise. Praṇatair abhigamyaṁ mūḍhair vedyam: only a devoted, surrendered soul is able to see God, while non-surrendered foolish people will forever be

Lord Nrisimhadeva manifesting from within the pillar

unable to understand Him. In fact, they consider themselves to be God and see everyone and everything with lusty eyes, judging them to be inferior.

In the Mathara Śruti and Śrīmad Bhāgavatam it is said: bhakty aham ekaya grahyaḥ bhaktir ebhainaṁ nayati, bhaktir ebhainaṁ darśayati. Bhakta Prahlad, his eyes tinged with love, could see that this wonderful form was the Supreme Lord Himself, while Hiraṇyakaśipu, blinded by lust, simply saw an amazing animal. The form of Nṛsiṁha was extremely frightening. He had eyes like shining gold and, with a growing anger and frowning brow, He was shaking His mane in a killing spree. His mouth gaped wide with sharp fangs and a sword-like tongue, roaring like a lion. His two paws were raised, His mouth and nostrils were open like mountain caves and His jaws looked very fierce and dangerous. His body touched the sky, His neck was thick and short, His thighs and chest were broad, His waist was thin and His body was covered with white hair shining like the moon. He had hundreds of arms, expanded everywhere, equipped with dangerous nails, conch-shell, disc, club, lotus and thunderbolt, which He was using to destroy the demons.

Śrī Hari is the greatest and most powerful magician and can assume any form. If He decides to kill someone, no one can oppose His unlimited power. However, despite seeing this amazing form of Nṛsiṁha, Hiraṇyakaśipu still believed himself to have some chance of defeating Him and, brandishing his mace, he rushed toward the Lord, roaring and thundering. Like a fly that falls into a fire, Hiraṇyakaśipu disappeared into the glaring light emanating from the body of Lord Nṛsiṁha. We should not doubt the validity of this description of the Bhāgavatam, because the Supreme Lord is supremely powerful and can perform any feat. At the beginning of creation, God destroys the deep darkness by

His own power. Therefore, it is not surprising that a dark demon can easily disappear into the pure sattvik light of Śrī Hari.

na tatra sūryo bhāti na candra-tārakaṁ
nemā vidyuto bhānti kuto 'yam agniḥ
tam eva bhāntam anubhāti sarvaṁ
tasya bhāsā sarvam idaṁ vibhāti
(Svetāśvatara Upaniṣad, 6.14)

With great anger and violence, Hiraṇyakaśipu attacked Lord Nṛsiṁha with his club, but the Lord responded with His own mace, as easily as Garuḍa devours a large snake.

A club, or mace, is a kind of heavy weapon usually made with iron. Fighting with clubs is indeed a dangerous duel. Among all the demigods, Vishnu, God, is the best fighter with the mace. The Vāyu Purāṇa explains the origin of the Lord's club. Once, there was a very fierce and dangerous demon named Gada, whose bones were harder and stronger than any weapon. He created a great disturbance for the demigods, so Brahmā went to him and asked him for his bones in charity. Later on, a mace was fashioned with Gada's bones, and offered to Vishnu. From this, the Lord derives His name as Gadādhara. In the Manvantara of Svayambhu, a son of Brahmā named Hetirakṣa obtained a boon from Brahmā and subsequently conquered the planetary system known as Svarga. All the demigods prayed to Vishnu for help, and Śrī Vishnu told them that He would defeat Hetirakṣa if the devas would give Him a suitable weapon. At that time, the devas used the bones of Gada to manufacture a strong mace and then offered it to the Lord, Who then killed Hetirakṣa but kept the weapon as His own. We can see from this example that a proud person is destroyed by his own pride, and that no one possesses any independent power, as God is the origin of all power.

Lord Nṛsiṁha stopped Hiraṇyakaśipu in his tracks with a blow of His mace. All the demigods, who had been driven out from Svarga by Hiraṇyakaśipu, gathered, and started to watch the fight from a hidden place. Just as Garuḍa sometimes plays with a snake before killing it, allowing it to escape from his mouth and then seizing it again, Lord Nṛsiṁha let the demon escape from His hands and the demigods became overwhelmed by fear. The great asura, thinking that Lord Nṛsiṁha was afraid of him, took a brief rest from the fight and then, with renewed energy, again attacked Him with sword and spear.

No one can oppose Śrī Hari. Nārāyaṇa, in the form of Nṛsiṁha, turned toward Hiraṇyakaśipu, who was laughing loudly while wielding his sword and spear. This demon had the power to move in the sky as though he were on the ground but the Lord caught him in the same way that a snake catches a mouse. The Lord tore apart the body of Hiraṇyakaśipu using only His own nails (and, therefore, without using any weapon), at dusk (which is neither day nor night), on the threshold of the assembly hall (which is neither indoors nor outdoors), by holding him on His lap (which is neither sky nor ground). Then He proceeded to rip out the demon's entrails and garland Himself with them, so that His white hair was completely drenched with blood. That form of Nṛsiṁha, with many arms and a terrible countenance, appeared extremely frightening. Finally the Lord plucked the heart out of Hiraṇyakaśipu's chest and turned to the many thousands of demons, who had rushed to fight Him with so many weapons, and killed them all with His nails only.

Exhibiting the triumphant behavior of a king who ascends the throne of a defeated enemy, the Lord sat on the siṁhāsana of Hiraṇyakaśipu. Nṛsiṁha Deva had feelings of deep affection

for His own servant, the gatekeeper of Vaikuṇṭha, who had taken a demon's body because of a curse. The Lord had liberated Hiraṇyakaśipu by slaying him, for everyone who is personally killed by the Lord attains salvation.

The Lord sat on the throne in the assembly hall, His face still frightening and angry in appearance. No one had the courage to approach Him to offer service. Hiraṇyakaśipu had been a burden for all the three worlds. Now that he had been killed, the wives of the demigods personally showered flowers from Svarga onto Nṛsiṁha Deva. Trying to pacify the anger of the Lord without getting too close to Him, all His servants and devotees such as Brahmā, Indra, Mahādeva, the Ṛṣis, Pitṛs, Siddhas, Vidyādharas, Nāgas, Manus, Apsarās, Gandharvas, Cāraṇas, Yakṣas, Kinnaras, Vaitālikas, Kimpuruṣas and others began to offer prayers.

the PRAYERS of the DEVAS

Śrī Brahmā said:

nato 'smy anantāya duranta-śaktaye
vicitra-vīryāya pavitra-karmaṇe
viśvasya sarga-sthiti-saṁyamān guṇaiḥ
sva-līlayā sandadhate 'vyayātmane
(Śrīmad Bhāgavatam, 7.8.40)

"You are unlimited. No one can understand You simply by means of knowledge. You possess amazing power and, although in Your wonderful pastimes You display anger, You are always situated in pure goodness. You are the cause of the creation, maintenance and destruction of the universe and You are indestructible spirit. Your appearance in this world is meant only to protect Your devotees."

Śrī Rudra said:

kopa-kālo yugāntas te
hato 'yam asuro 'lpakaḥ
tat-sutam pāhy upasṛtaṁ
bhaktaṁ te bhakta-vatsala
(Śrīmad Bhāgavatam, 7.8.41)

"At the end of the day of Brahmā comes the time for destruction. At that time You manifest Your wrath. Because of affection for Your devotee, Prahlad, You have manifested that same anger. Now that this insignificant demon is dead, You may subdue Your anger. Please protect Your surrendered devotee, Prahlad, the son of Hiraṇyakaśipu."

The associates of Vishnu said:

adyaitad dhari-nara-rūpam adbhutaṁ te
dṛṣṭaṁ naḥ śaraṇada sarva-loka-śarma
so 'yaṁ te vidhikara īśa vipra-śaptas
tasyedaṁ nidhanam anugrahāya vidmaḥ
(Śrīmad Bhāgavatam, 7.8.56)

"O protector of the surrendered souls, today we have seen Your extraordinary form of Nṛsiṁha, which is perfectly auspicious. This demon Hiraṇyakaśipu was Your former servant, who had been cursed by the brāhmaṇas to take a demon's body. Now You have shown him great mercy by killing him."

Some of the prayers offered contained expressions of personal pleasure, because the persons who offered them to the Lord had finally obtained what they had desired.

The Pitṛs said, "This demon had been snatching away our share of the oblations offered by our descendents and the sesame water offered to us at places of pilgrimage. Using His nails, Lord Nṛsiṁha tore his belly apart and gave us back that which was intended for us. We are therefore offering our obeisances to Nṛsiṁha Deva."

The Siddhas said, "This evil rogue had taken away the fruits of our tapasya and yoga-siddhis [such as anima, mahimā, etc.]. Now You have ripped apart this miscreant with Your nails. O Lord Nṛsiṁha, we offer You our respectful obeisances."

The Vidyādharas said, "This foolish demon, proud of his own abilities and powers, had been hampering our mystic powers, by which we used to appear and disappear at will. Now You have killed this demon like an animal. O our Lord Nṛsiṁha, we are eternally offering You our respect."

The Yakṣas said, "We are generally thought to occupy a high position among Your servants, but this son of Diti, Hiraṇyakaśipu, engaged us in the menial work of carrying his palanquin in order to humiliate us. After coming to know of this insult, You killed him."

The Kinnaras said, "O Lord, we are Your devoted followers, but this demon was engaging us in his service without any remuneration. Because of that sin, that demon was killed by You. O Lord! You have given us unlimited pleasure."

Despite the many prayers of Brahmā and the demigods, the Lord's anger did not seem to subside. So, all the demigods approached Śrī Lakṣmī Devī for help. The Goddess of Fortune, the eternal consort of Nārāyaṇa, was extremely frightened and could not muster the courage to approach the Lord. Then Brahmā, with the intent of placating the Lord's anger, asked Prahlad to approach the Lord. Like a cub of a lioness who slowly approaches his mother without any fear, Prahlad approached Lord Nṛsiṁha on the order of Brahmā. He offered his aṣṭāṅga daṇḍavat praṇāma by prostrating on the ground, while keeping his folded hands over his head.

ugro 'py anugra evāyaṁ
sva-bhaktānāṁ nṛkeśarī
keśarīva sva-potānām
anyeṣām ugra-vikramaḥ
(Śrī Caitanya Caritāmṛta, Madhya-līlā, 8.6)

"A lioness is usually very ferocious by nature, but she is always sweet and tender to her children. In the same way Lord Nṛsiṁha, who exhibited a terrible wrath toward the demons, shows great affection for His devotees, such as Prahlad."

The Lord, Who is also called bhakta-vatsala, "very affectionate to His devotees", saw Prahlad prostrated at His lotus feet. Out of affection He put His lotus hands, which are so very difficult to attain, on Prahlad's head. The touch of those lotus hands of Lord Nṛsiṁha at once removed all the impurities connected with Prahlad's taking birth in a demon's family, and the child was overcome by symptoms of deep love. Prahlad started to offer beautiful prayers, explaining the true nature of the appearance of Lord Nṛsiṁha. In this way, the Lord induced Prahlad to speak about His glories.

the PRAYER of PRAHLAD

Śrī Prahlad said:

brahmādayaḥ sura-gaṇā munayo 'tha siddhāḥ
sattvaikatāna-gatayo vacasāṁ pravāhaiḥ
nārādhituṁ puru-guṇair adhunāpi pipruḥ
kiṁ toṣṭum arhati sa me harir ugra-jāteḥ
(Śrīmad Bhāgavatam, 7.9.8)

"O Lord Nṛsiṁha, what qualities did You see in me that You wished to bless me? The truth about You and the meaning of Your manifestation are extremely complex and difficult to know. All the demigods, beginning with Brahmā, and all the Ṛṣis and Siddhas, who are extremely elevated in sattva-guṇa and in the practice of dharma, jñāna and tapasya, finding pleasure in the higher levels of existence, have not yet been able to please You with many wonderfully elaborate prayers. How is someone like me, devoid of all knowledge and living in darkness, born in an āsurik family, able to please You with prayers?"

manye dhanābhijana-rūpa-tapaḥ-śrutaujas-
tejaḥ-prabhāva-bala-pauruṣa-buddhi-yogāḥ

nārādhanāya hi bhavanti parasya puṁso
bhaktyā tutoṣa bhagavān gaja-yūtha-pāya
(Śrīmad Bhāgavatam, 7.9.9)

"Therefore, I think You will not be pleased by wealth [dhana], good family [abhijana], beauty [rūpa], penance [tapasya], scriptural knowledge [śruta], sense control [ojaḥ], luster [tejaḥ], power [prabhāva], physical strength [bala], vitality [pauruṣa], intelligence [buddhi], and mystic power [yoga other than bhakti]. Gajendra had no such qualifications, not even prosperity, yet by pure and simple bhakti he could please the Lord. My only asset is the causeless mercy of Your dear devotee, Nārada Muni, who gave me a drop of devotion."

viprād dvi-ṣaḍ-guṇa-yutād aravinda nābha-
pādāravinda-vimukhāt śvapacaṁ variṣṭham
manye tad-arpita-mano-vacanehitārtha-
prāṇaṁ punāti sa kulaṁ na tu bhūrimānaḥ
(Śrīmad Bhāgavatam, 7.9.10)

The Mahābhārata describes the twelve qualities of the brāhmaṇa as: following religious principles, speaking truthfully, controlling the senses by undergoing austerities and penances, being free from jealousy, being intelligent, being tolerant, creating no enemies, performing yajña, giving charity, being steady, being well-versed in śāstra and observing vows.

jñānaṁ ca satyaṁ ca damaḥ śrutaṁ ca
hy amātsaryaṁ hrīs titikṣānasūyā
yajñaś ca dānaṁ ca dhṛtiḥ ca śamaś ca
mahā-vratā dvādaśa brāhmaṇasya
(Sanat-sujāta)

If a brāhmaṇa (and what to speak of a kṣatriya, vaiśya or śūdra), possessing all these twelve qualities, is not dedicated to the lotus feet of the Lord, he is lower than a person who has become a sincere devotee even though that devotee may have taken birth in a family of dog eaters (caṇḍālas). In fact, a devotee is the most qualified person because he is dedicating everything he possesses to the service of Hari, including his mind, words, activities, wealth, property, and his very life itself. Not only is such a devotee completely purified, but he also purifies his family. On the other hand, a brāhmaṇa, who possesses the twelve qualities but is not interested in devotion to the Lord, will be unable even to purify himself, what to speak of purifying his family.

Lord Mahādeva told his wife Sati:

vidyā-tapo-vitta-vapur-vayaḥ-kulaiḥ
satāṁ guṇaiḥ ṣaḍbhir asattametaraiḥ
smṛtau hatāyāṁ bhṛta-māna-durdṛśaḥ
stabdhā na paśyanti hi dhāma bhūyasām
(Śrīmad Bhāgavatam, 4.3.17)

"Knowledge, austerity, wealth, attractive appearance, youth and good fortune are very exalted qualities in a sādhu, but they produce the opposite result when they are possessed by unholy persons. Such impious people actually become puffed up with their own pride because of these qualities and very soon their intelligence and discrimination disappear, so much so that they are not even able to see the qualities of the great devotees."

naivātmanaḥ prabhur ayaṁ nija-lābha-pūrṇo
mānaṁ janād aviduṣaḥ karuṇo vṛṇīte

yad yaj jano bhagavate vidadhīta mānaṁ
tac cātmane prati-mukhasya yathā mukha-śrīḥ
(Śrīmad Bhāgavatam, 7.9.11)

"The Lord is not satisfied by one who simply performs tapasya. On the contrary, He is very pleased when someone offers Him respect and worship by chanting and speaking about His Names, Qualities, Forms and Pastimes."

One may object that the Lord seems selfish. "Will He not be pleased unless offered some bribe?" Prahlad Maharaj answers this by saying, "On the contrary, God is eternally satisfied in Himself and does not need anything. Nothing is outside Him and no one is separate from Him. Rather, all is eternally contained in Him and under His full control. It is not possible for the infinitesimal living entity, who possesses nothing independently, to attract the Lord by offering something He does not already have. Even the person who is offering something to the Lord is also within Him. God is the only one who possesses full and complete knowledge, and He accepts respect from the ignorant out of His mercy. If He were not to accept their worship, how would they be able to improve their good qualities and attain purification? If one were to see the reflection of his face in a mirror and wished to improve the beauty of that reflection, he would need to tend to the face itself—it could not be otherwise. This body is like a mirror and, by increasing one's spiritual power, the beneficial effects upon the body will increase. This is possible only by means of service to God, and not otherwise. By respectfully offering worship to the Lord, we will also be glorified. By speaking about Your glories, although I have no qualifications, I am also obtaining great benefit.

"Brahmā and all the demigods are extremely qualified in sattva-guṇa, but they always remain under Your control like servants and followers. Please be satisfied with us, who are also Your followers and servants, although tainted by the qualities of rajas and tamas. You manifest to give happiness to Your devotees, to engage in wonderful pastimes and to benefit the whole world. Now the cause of Your anger has gone: Hiraṇyakaśipu is dead, killed by You. Everyone is happy when a snake or scorpion is killed. By Your appearance, You have given unlimited happiness to all good and saintly people, so I am praying that You will please terminate Your pastime of anger. By simply remembering You, all fears are destroyed. So why should one be frightened of You? Actually, I do not feel afraid at all when I see Your ferocious face. In my opinion, material existence is the real cause of fear. Those who are not engaged in Your pure devotional service and are hostile toward You, trying to fight You, are falling into the miseries of material existence. But Your lotus feet are a safe and happy shelter, the only way to attain liberation from the cycle of birth and death.

"Suffering comes from contact with things we do not want and not obtaining what we do want, while pleasure is just the opposite (obtaining what we want and avoiding what we do not want). One can only increase his sufferings if he tries to solve his miseries by becoming averse to devotion to the Lord. The only way to remove all suffering is by means of service to Your lotus feet. I pray to You to kindly give me such service. You are the Supreme Lord and the best friend and well-wisher of everyone—the dearest and most beloved of all. We will be able to overcome the ocean of suffering, which is only due to separation from You, by following Your devotees who serve Your lotus feet. A boat is not a real shelter for a drowning man, parents are not the real shelter for their children and medicine is not the real shelter for a patient. Although they seem to represent safety and protection, they are not able to vanquish all suffering in the same way that taking shelter of Your lotus feet can.

"Whatever happens in this world happens by Your will. Everything is an instrument of Your plan, used by You to protect and take care of us. The external energy with its six transformations is Your energy only, and from this external energy desire is produced. From desire, which is very difficult to overcome, the subtle body is developed. But You are above all this, above māyā, the illusory external energy. You are situated in Your internal energy, known as svarūpa-śakti. You are the only one who can offer protection from the onslaught of the external potency and from all living entities, who belong to Your marginal potency.

"I am taking shelter at Your lotus feet, which liberate one from all fears. Please lift me up to that position at Your lotus feet. Those who desire to enjoy the pleasures of Svarga and other forms of material sense gratification might think that their goal is the highest, but I have directly seen the result of attaining the heavenly planets. My father conquered the supreme position in Svarga by simply displaying an angry look, but now he has been killed by Your hands. You are the only Supreme Lord, therefore I am not asking from You the position of Dhruva, nor to be the supreme governor of the universe or similar things which will be finished in time. This material body is the cause of unlimited suffering, disease, etc. Those who are wise and learned reach this conclusion but, due to their attachment to māyā, they cannot really understand, as they are unable to become free from material desire.

"Desire is like fire. By feeding it, we make it grow more and more and become scorched by the three kinds of sufferings (ādhyātmika kleśa, those created by our own body and mind; ādhibhautika kleśa, those created by other living entities and ādhidaivika kleśa, those created by nature, such as floods, earthquakes etc.). Having taken birth in a very degraded family of demons, I am steeped in the lower influences of rajas and tamas and my position is extremely bad. Yet, in Your unlimited mercy, You chose to bless this poor wretch by putting Your lotus hand on my head, something that is difficult to obtain even by Brahmā, Rudra or Lakṣmī Devī. You do not discriminate between higher and lower, and You shower Your blessings equally everywhere. Like a desire tree, You fulfill all the desires of all living entities and, because of their sincere worship, reciprocate with them by giving them whatever they need.

"I was living in a pit full of snakes [attachment to material objects, which is extremely poisonous], but, by the will of Providence and by the mercy of Your devotee and personal associate, Śrī Devārṣi Nārada, You kindly accepted me as Your servant. I will never be able to forget the affection and causeless mercy I received from Your devotee, Nārada. The lotus feet of my spiritual master are my eternal objects of worship. You protected me because of my association with Your pure devotee and, for the same reason, You killed my father. By doing so, You were not taking sides by defending me against my father, because You are the Supreme Whole and nothing is outside of You. Everything rests in You only. Before the creation, You existed. During the maintenance of creation, everything exists in You only, and after the creation is rewound You will continue to exist as before.

"The universe is created, maintained and destroyed by Your māyā-śakti, which is composed of the three guṇas and works as an instrument of Your supreme will. While the conditioned souls are confused by duality, You are always untouched by the three guṇas, in spite of being their origin. Although You are everywhere, You are also not everywhere. You are inconceivable, beyond the three normal states of consciousness of the living entities [wakefulness, dream and deep sleep], in a constant state of super-consciousness.

"At the time of annihilation, You lay down on the Kāraṇa Ocean and, when You wished to create the world of māyā again, from Your navel sprouted a lotus flower on which Brahmā appeared. For a thousand celestial years Brahmā tried to understand himself by means of his senses and material body, but without success. Only when Brahmā started to meditate, concentrating inward, did his consciousness and heart become purified, enabling him to catch a glimpse of You. By Your mercy, he was finally able to see Your wonderful form, displaying thousands of arms and legs [the virāṭa-purūṣa] and felt a great happiness.

"In the form of Hayagrīva, You killed the two demons, Madhu and Kaiṭabha, and rescued the Vedas from the ocean of destruction, delivering them to Brahmā. Your advent is always meant to destroy evil and to protect the good."

itthaṁ nṛ-tiryag-ṛṣi-deva-jhaṣāvatārair
lokān vibhāvayasi haṁsi jagat pratīpān
dharmaṁ mahā-puruṣa pāsi yugānuvṛttaṁ
channaḥ kalau yad abhavas tri-yugo 'tha sa tvam
(Śrīmad Bhāgavatam, 7.9.38)

"In this way, You appear among human beings, animals, ṛṣis, demigods and even among fish. By these avatāras You constantly take care of the three worlds, destroying their enemies. O Supreme Personality of Godhead, You regularly descend in every yuga to protect dharma. In Kali Yuga Your avatāra is concealed and, therefore, You are called 'Tri-yuga'."

The Lord descends in Satya, Tretā and Dvāpara Yugas to destroy the demons. During the reign of Vaivasvata Manu, at the end of Dvāpara Yuga, the Lord Almighty appears directly as Śrī

Krishna and, in the next Kali Yuga, He appears as Śrī Gaurāṅga Mahāprabhu, filled with the deep emotions of rādhā-bhāva. Śrī Gaurāṅga Mahāprabhu, the personification of extraordinary magnanimity, did not kill the bad, but rather, He destroyed their bad nature by giving them the Name of God and inspiring them to love the Lord. He was not carrying weapons to kill the asuras as in the other three yugas because, in Kali Yuga, God does not fully manifest Himself and therefore He is not recognized by everyone. For this reason the Lord is called Tri-yuga, indicating that in Kali Yuga there is no līlā-avatāra.

naitan manas tava kathāsu vikuṇṭha-nātha
samprīyate durita-duṣṭam asādhu tīvram
kāmāturaṁ harṣa-śoka-bhayaiṣaṇārtaṁ
tasmin kathaṁ tava gatiṁ vimṛśāmi dīnaḥ
(Śrīmad Bhāgavatam, 7.9.39)

"Due to my misfortune, I have no taste for listening to and reciting Your sweet pastimes as the various avatāras, and instead I am haunted by worries, sorrow, mourning, loss and thoughts of wealth."

jihvaikato 'cyuta vikarṣati māvitṛptā
śiśno 'nyatas tvag-udaraṁ śravaṇaṁ kutaścit
ghrāṇo 'nyataś capala-dṛk kva ca karma-śaktir
bahvyaḥ sapatnya iva geha-patiṁ lunanti
(Śrīmad Bhāgavatam, 7.9.40)

"Like a man who has many wives is sometimes pulled here and there to take care of different things, I am pulled here and there by my insatiable senses. The tongue is there on one side, the genitals on another. The skin wants to experience objects nice to the touch, while the belly wants to be filled with good foodstuffs and the ears want to hear beautiful tunes. My restless eyes are always looking in various directions to detect pleasing sights, and the senses of action [karma-indriyas, such as the hands, legs, etc.] also pull me in various directions. I am being torn apart by them, O Acyuta! O Nṛsiṁha, You are so merciful! Demoniac people are blinded by the spell of māyā. Their vision of life is absorbed by the idea of enemies and friends and they are consumed by the fire of the three types of suffering. Please lift up these demons, who are covered by the deep darkness of ignorance. For You, nothing is impossible. Since You are the cause of birth, life and death of the living entities, You can also elevate them."

After listening to the prayers of Prahlad Maharaj, Nṛsiṁha Deva asked, "Dear Prahlad, you are such a young boy—only five years old. Why should you worry so much about elevating others? The munis will take care of such matters."

prāyeṇa deva munayaḥ sva-vimukti-kāmā
maunaṁ caranti vijane na parārtha-niṣṭhāḥ
naitān vihāya kṛpaṇān vimumukṣa eko
nānyaṁ tvad asya śaraṇaṁ bhramato 'nupaśye
(Śrīmad Bhāgavatam, 7.9.44)

Prahlad replied, "O Lord, many great sages observe vows and reside in solitary places. They are only interested in their own liberation and they are not interested in the fate of others. I do not wish to attain liberation for myself, if these poor souls must be left behind. Except for You, I cannot see anyone who can protect the bewildered souls, who suffer in the cycle of birth and death."

Lord Nṛsiṁha Deva again objected: "Those for whom you are worrying so much do not want to be liberated. Actually, they think that material enjoyment is very nice—the best way of life for them. Why are you unnecessarily thinking about them? The sages engage in tapasya to attain the object of their desire and so should other people. You can tell all these others that they should also engage in tapasya."

yan maithunādi-gṛhamedhi-sukhaṁ hi tucchaṁ
kaṇḍūyanena karayor iva duḥkha-duḥkham
tṛpyanti neha kṛpaṇā bahu-duḥkha-bhājaḥ
kaṇḍūtivan manasijaṁ viṣaheta dhīraḥ
(Śrīmad Bhāgavatam, 7.9.45)

Prahlad answered, "Asuras are very foolish and they are convinced that the greatest possible pleasure is to have sex, which is exactly like the illusory pleasure of scratching the skin to relieve itching. The itching will only get worse. It is not real happiness, but just suffering. This idea of material enjoyment is false and illusory, created by māyā.

"The gṛhamedhis, those who are deeply attached to family life, seek their enjoyment on a low platform of sensual pleasure. When the skin itches, one rubs the two hands together to relieve the irritation, but this ultimately aggravates the situation and enjoyment becomes suffering. A lusty person will not be able to get full satisfaction in family pleasures, even after enduring great difficulties and suffering. Some intelligent people, however, are able to tolerate this itching, which is lusty desire, by taking shelter of tapasya, the study of the Vedas and the observance of mauna-vrata [the vow of silence], but this will be possible only by the mercy of the Lord. Because the demons are unable to control their senses, they will not be able to engage in tapasya properly, so, if they are taught to observe tapasya and vratas, they will just use such things as a source of income and, because they are very proud, they will not even be able to get any material benefit. O Nṛsiṁha Deva, one can attain You only by means of bhakti-yoga [devotional service] and not by vratas and tapasya. You are everywhere, but you are not easy to see, just as fire is contained in firewood but is invisible to those who have no knowledge."

bhaktyāham ekayā grāhyaḥ
praśrayātmā priyaḥ satām
bhaktiḥ punāti man-niṣṭhā
śvapākān api sambhavāt
(Śrīmad Bhāgavatam, 11.14.21)

"The sādhus can attain Me, the Supreme Soul and supreme object of love, only by the potency of bhakti, pure devotion supported by full faith. Pure, concentrated devotion can purify even a caṇḍāla."

"The munis who are situated in the jñāna-mārga and who follow a sādhana based upon tapasya, vratas and study of the scriptures, will ultimately fail to attain You and all their efforts will be vain."

jñāne prayāsam udapāsya namanta eva
jīvanti san-mukharitāṁ bhavadīya-vārtām
sthāne sthitāḥ śruti-gatāṁ tanu-vāṅ-manobhir
ye prāyaśo 'jita jito 'py asi tais tri-lokyām
(Śrīmad Bhāgavatam, 10.14.3)

bahūnāṁ janmanām ante
jñānavān māṁ prapadyate
vāsudevaḥ sarvam iti
sa mahātmā su-durlabhaḥ
(Bhagavad-gītā, 7.19)

tat te 'rhattama namaḥ stuti-karma-pujaḥ
karma smṛtiś caraṇayoḥ śravaṇaṁ kathāyām
saṁsevayā tvayi vineti ṣaḍ-aṅgayā kiṁ
bhaktiṁ janaḥ paramahaṁsa-gatau labheta
(Śrīmad Bhāgavatam, 7.9.50)

"Therefore, O Supremely Worshipable Person, I offer my obeisances unto You. Without accepting the six paths of devotion—praying to You, offering all one's activities to You, worshiping You, working on Your behalf, remembering Your lotus feet, and listening to the narrations of Your pastimes—how will it be possible to develop pure devotion for You as the paramahaṁsa devotee does? While everyone is qualified to accept bhagavata-dharma, devotional service to the Lord, not everyone is qualified to practice the study of the Vedas, tapasya and vratas. However, even after achieving success in these practices, one will still not be able to attain You. On the other hand, by the practice of bhakti, the devotees, who are surrendered souls, will obtain the eternal fruits of devotion. As secondary effects they will get relief from the sufferings of material existence and liberation. My great fortune is that, after obtaining the service of Your devotee, I lost all desire to attain anything else."

Lord Nṛsiṁha Deva, who is very affectionate to His devotees and Who manifested this angry pastime to punish those who were harassing His devotee, was extremely pleased by the prayers of Prahlad. Seeing that Prahlad was happy and content, His anger subsided. He smiled and offered to give Prahlad whatever boon he desired.

"Dear boy, may you live long! No one can see Me if I am not pleased. The pleasure of attaining My darśana will wash away all suffering and anxiety. For this reason, the sādhus, who wish to obtain real happiness, always strive to please Me. You may now ask for any boon you desire."

The Lord is also called bhakta-vatsala (very affectionate to His devotees) and paramodara (most magnanimous). One should not be ashamed to ask Him for a boon. However, Prahlad was not interested in any boon. he had no other desire because he had already obtained a taste of the nectar of pure devotion to God.

ekāntino yasya na kañcanārthaṁ
vāñchanti ye vai bhagavat-prapannāḥ
aty-adbhutaṁ tac-caritaṁ sumaṅgalaṁ
gāyanta ānanda-samudra-magnāḥ
(Śrīmad Bhāgavatam, 8.3.20)

"Those who are completely surrendered to the Lord obtain relief from all kinds of material desire and enter into an ocean of happiness and attachment by chanting and singing the glories of the auspicious character of Śrī Krishna, His wonderful Qualities, Forms, Names and pastimes."

Young Prahlad realized that, due to his birth, material blessings may have disturbed his devotion to the Lord, and he replied with a smile, "O Lord, I already have many desires by nature. Please do not increase my greed with material boons. I am surrendered unto You."

Śrī Nṛsiṁha Deva said, "I have no intention of increasing material greed in My devotee; rather, I have offered a boon to show the whole world the extraordinary qualities of My devotees. Everyone should see what the thoughts and symptoms of My servants are. They are so free from all material desires that they will not even ask for a boon when they are offered one."

Prahlad said:

nānyathā te 'khila-guro
ghaṭeta karuṇātmanaḥ
yas ta āśiṣa āśāste
na sa bhṛtyaḥ sa vai vaṇik
(Śrīmad Bhāgavatam, 7.10.4)

"O Nṛsiṁha Deva, You are the Universal Spiritual Master, extremely merciful, and You wish to offer a boon to Your devotee to test his sincerity and to glorify him. Those who pray to You for material benefits are not really Your devotees. They are just interested in making a business deal with You. A servant who asks for something in exchange of service is not really a servant, and a master who demands respect from his servants is not really a master. I am simply Your devotee and You are my Lord and Master—not on the temporary material platform, but on the eternal transcendental platform. Our relationship is completely different from the material service given by subjects to a king."

Śrī Nṛsiṁha Deva said, "Dear Prahlad, if you don't accept a boon from Me, My fame will be tainted, because I am known as the greatest among those who give boons."

Prahlad Maharaj replied, "Surely, O most generous Supreme Personality of Godhead, I do not want Your name and fame to be tainted. If my refusal will cast any doubt upon Your munificence, then please grant me this boon, that I will never desire to ask for any boon because, when greed arises, everything is destroyed: the senses, mind, life force and body, dharma, tolerance, intelligence, shame, wealth, power, memory and truthfulness. O lotus-eyed Lord, one who gives up all kinds of desire becomes entitled to attain the same opulence You have. You are the form of the Supreme Brahman, endowed with all six opulences (wealth, beauty, fame, power, wisdom and renunciation). You are the Lord Who removes all suffering and obstacles on the path of devotion. I offer my obeisances unto You."

Pleased by the words of Prahlad, Nṛsiṁha Deva said, "My pure and faithful devotee never asks for personal enjoyment in this life or in the next. Nonetheless, you will become the king of the Daityas and have all material enjoyment, up to the end of the life of Manu. Giving up the Vedic karma-kāṇḍa (material religiosity intended to obtain fruitive results) and all social attachment, you will worship Me through bhakti-yoga. When the results of your previous activities are exhausted, you will be free from the bondage of all good and bad karma and you will become a sādhana-siddha, in the association of great and perfect personalities like Nārada."

Śrīla Viśvanātha Cakravartī comments, "evam prahlādasya amsena sādhana siddhatvam nityā siddhatvam ca nārada adi bajjñayam." Although Prahlad Maharaj fully accepted the decision of Lord Nṛsiṁha Deva, he prayed to the Lord in favor of his father. At the time of death, his father, Hiraṇyakaśipu, was in the direct presence of Nṛsiṁha Deva and was, therefore, already purified. Yet, he had not been able to realize the supreme opulence and divinity of the Lord, because he falsely considered Him as the killer of his brother Hiraṇyakṣa and felt deep enmity toward Him. He had also kicked Nṛsiṁha Deva with his feet and had harassed Prahlad for being His devotee and worshiping Him. So Prahlad prayed to Lord Nṛsiṁha Deva to forgive Hiraṇyakaśipu for these serious offenses.

Again Nṛsiṁha Deva told Prahlad, "Beloved Prahlad, you do not need to pray to Me to purify your father from all sins. Those who live in hell are liberated simply by remembering Me. Because your father could see Me directly at the time of his death and because he touched Me during the fight and was even taken on My lap when I tore apart his belly and garlanded Myself with his intestines, he cannot be impure. Even the parents who gave birth to you in the previous twenty-one lifetimes have been liberated."

triḥ-saptabhiḥ pitā pūtaḥ
pitṛbhiḥ saha te 'nagha
yat sādho 'sya kule jāto
bhavān vai kula-pāvanaḥ
(Śrīmad Bhāgavatam, 7.10.18)

"O Anagha, O saintly personality free from all sins, twenty-one families into which you were previously born have been liberated because you have purified those parents by being born from them."

In the case of Prahlad, his parents from the last twenty-one lives were purified. This does not indicate twenty-one generations of Prahlad's ancestors, but the parents of Prahlad in each of his previous twenty-one lifetimes—all those who had directly served him. Śrī Madhvācārya comments, "janmāntara pitribhis tri-saptabhiḥ."

Nṛsiṁha Deva continued to glorify His devotees, explaining that even unholy places will be purified if sādhus, who possess equal vision, are self-satisfied and practice sadācara, choose to reside there. Those who are practically situated in pure devotion, and are free from any tinge of material desire, have no hostility toward any living entity and do not consider them to be either good or bad. The example demonstrated by Prahlad shows that he is the greatest of all devotees.

kuru tvaṁ preta-kṛtyāni
pituḥ pūtasya sarvaśaḥ

mad-aṅga-sparśanenāṅga
lokān yāsyati suprajāḥ
(Śrīmad Bhāgavatam, 7.10.22)

"My dear child, simply by touching My body your father became completely purified. Nevertheless, you should execute whatever ceremonies are necessary as per the social rules."

Śrīla Viśvanātha Cakravartī comments, "mad āṅga sparsanena eva sarvasyaḥ putasya te pituḥ pāpa samkaiva nasti, tad api pretakaryyani pretasya eva krityani kuru kevalam vyavahara rakshartham iti arthaḥ." A surrendered soul, a devotee of Śrī Hari, who practically engages in pure devotional service for the pleasure of the Lord, automatically executes all his duties to his father and mother, demigods, goddesses, ṛṣis, human beings and all other living entities. Therefore, they are not dependent upon anyone and do not owe anything to anyone. A pure devotee does not need to execute any of the duties prescribed in the karma-kāṇḍa, such as śraddha (funeral rites) or other similar ceremonies, but they might perform such activities, according to the law, so as to maintain order and balance in society.

Śrī Nṛsiṁha Deva said, "Under My order, you will ascend the throne of your father and perform all activities prescribed in the Vedas, while remembering Me at the same time."

Śrīla Viśvanātha Cakravartī comments: "yadyapi mad bhaktasya tava nasti karma adhikāras tad api mat ajñayaiva vyavahara rakṣārtham karmani kuru." According to the order of Lord Śrī Nṛsiṁha Deva, Prahlad Maharaj completed all the necessary funeral rites for his father with the help of the brāhmaṇas. Brahmā, surrounded by all the demigods, observed that Lord Nṛsiṁha Deva's anger had subsided and he approached the Lord to offer many sincere prayers.

Brahmā prayed: "O ultimate goal of all living entities! This Hiraṇyakaśipu had become a great disturbance for the whole universe, but he was killed by You. We consider ourselves blessed by Your grace. This demon could not be killed by any living entity created by me. After receiving a boon from me, pride swallowed him and he started to destroy all pious activities prescribed in the Vedas. By our good fortune, You have protected the young son of Hiraṇyakaśipu, Prahlad, who is a soul completely surrendered unto You. O Lord, if someone meditates on Your form of Nṛsiṁha Deva, he will be relieved from all kinds of fear and from imminent death." Lord Nṛsiṁha Deva told Brahmā that the giving of such boons to demons, who are very cruel by nature, is a mistake comparable to giving nectar to poisonous snakes.

After being worshiped by Brahmā, the transcendental Lord disappeared. Prahlad Maharaj offered his prayers and worship to Brahmā, Mahādeva, the Prajāpatis and the demigods. Finally, after consulting Śukrācārya and the munis, Brahmā crowned Prahlad as the lord of the Daityas and Dānavas. After blessing Prahlad, Brahmā and all the inhabitants of the higher planets returned to their own abodes.

the Glories of Hearing Prahlad Caritra

From the holy life of Prahlad, we can learn the meaning of bhagavata-dharma, devotional service to the Lord, by which one can attain the Supreme Personality of Godhead. Someone who hears, reads or recites the holy description of the supreme potency of Lord Vishnu with faith will become liberated from the bondage of karma. Anyone who hears or reads, with full attention, this pastime of Lord Vishnu,

Who in His form of Nṛsiṁha killed the lord of the demons, will become free from all fears and ultimately attain Vaikuṇṭha-dhāma, the transcendental abode of the Lord.

ei mata prabhu priyā gadādhara saṅge
tana mukhe bhagavata suni thake raṅge
gadādhara pādena sammukhe bhagavata
suniya prakase prabhu prema bhava yata

prahlāda-caritra ara dhruvera caritra
satavritti kariya sunena saba hita
ara karyye prabhura nahika avasara
nāma guṇa balena sunena nirantara
(Caitanya Bhagavata, Antya-līlā, 10.32-35)

"The holy life of Prahlad is described in the Seventh Canto of Śrīmad Bhāgavatam, while that of Dhruva is narrated in the Fourth Canto. Śrī Gadādhara Pandit used to give discourses on these pastimes by reading from Śrīmad Bhāgavatam. Śrī Gaurasundara used to listen to Śrī Gadādhara's description of the devotional practices of Prahlad and Dhruva hundreds of times with great attention."

adhāma kulete yadi viṣṇu bhakta haya
tathāpi sei se pūjya sarvaśāstre kaya
uttama kulete janmi śrī kṛṣṇe na bhaje
kule tāra ki karibe narakete maje

ei saba vedavakyera sakśi dekhaite
janmilena haridāsa adhāma kulete
prahlāda ye hena daitya, kapi haṇumān
ei mata haridāsa nica jati nāma
(Caitanya Bhagavata, Ādi-līlā, 16.238-241)

During His travels in South India, Śrī Mahāprabhu visited the top of Mount Simhacala. After taking darśana of the Deity of Jiyada Nṛsiṁha, He danced, prayed and sang for a long time, "Śrī nṛsiṁha, jaya nṛsiṁha, jaya jaya nṛsiṁha, prahlādeśa jaya jaya padmā-mukha padmā-bhṛnga."

ugro 'py anugra evāyaṁ
sva-bhaktānāṁ nṛkeśarī
keśarīva sva-potānām
anyeṣām ugra-vikramaḥ
(Caitanya Caritāmṛta, Madhya-līlā, 8.6)

"A lioness is extremely ferocious, yet she will show completely opposite behavior toward her child. Likewise, although Lord Nṛsiṁha is very dangerous for the demons such as Hiraṇyakaśipu, He is full of affection for His devotees such as Prahlad."

Śrī Nṛsiṁha is residing in the heart of every living entity, and from there He can destroy the demons of desire for wealth, sex, and fame (kanaka, kāmini and pratiṣṭha). As a result, devotion to the Lord will be established and increased, which is the inner nature of the spirit soul.

the END

The holy life of Prahlad is also described in Harivaṁsa, Brihan Nāradīya Purāṇa and Hari-bhakti-vilāsa (which is considered the Vaiṣṇava smṛti). All these scriptures explain how Prahlad attained devotion to the lotus feet of Lord Nṛsiṁha Deva.

Nṛsiṁha Deva told Prahlad:

"In ancient times, in the place known as Avanti Nagar, lived a brāhmaṇa, expert in the Vedas, whose name was Vasu Sharma. His wife, Suhila, had all the qualities of a sādhu, a peaceful nature and natural devotion to her husband and, due to possessing all these qualities, she had become famous in the three worlds. Vasu Sharma begot five sons in the womb of Suhila, four of whom were very good and well behaved. They were full of many desirable qualities and were respectful to their father. However, the eldest son (who was, in fact, you in a previous life) was attracted to prostitutes and, as a result, lost his character. In that life, your name was Vāsudeva. By the association of a prostitute, you lost all your good qualities. On the day of Nṛsiṁha caturdaśī, because of a quarrel with that prostitute, you both fasted and passed the night without sleeping and, in this way, you unknowingly obtained the result of observing the Nṛsiṁha caturdaśī-vrata. The prostitute ascended to heaven and, in the form of an Apsara, enjoyed many pleasures but, in the end, she became My beloved devotee. In the same way, you also took birth as the son of Hiraṇyakaśipu and became My beloved devotee. By observing Nṛsiṁha caturdaśī-vrata, Brahmā obtains the power of creation and Śiva obtains the power of destruction. By observance of this vow, everyone can obtain any kind of power and all their desires will be fulfilled."

Sanskrit Pronunciation Guide

Vowels

a—like the *a* in org*a*n or the *u* in b*u*t
ā—like the *a* in f*a*r, but held twice as long as short *a*
i—like the *i* in p*i*n
ī—like the *i* in p*i*que, but held twice as long as short *i*
u—like the *u* in p*u*sh
ū—like the *u* in r*u*le, but held twice as long as short *u*
ṛ—like *ree* in *ree*d
ḷ—like *l* followed by *ṛ* (*lṛ*)
e—like the *e* in th*e*y
ai—like the *ai* in *ai*sle
o—like the *o* in g*o*
au—like the *ow* in h*ow*

Consonants

k—as in *k*ite
kh—as in Ec*kh*art
g—as in *g*ive
gh—as in di*g-h*ard
ṅ—as in si*ng*
c—as in *ch*air
j—as in *j*oy
jh—as in he*dgeh*og
ñ—as in ca*ny*on
ṭ—as in *t*ub, but with tongue against the roof of the mouth
ṭh—as in ligh*t-h*eart, but with tongue against the roof of the mouth
d—as in *d*ove, but with tongue against the teeth
ḍ—as in *d*ove, but with tongue against the roof of the mouth
dh—as in re*d-h*ot, but with tongue against the teeth
ḍh—as in re*d-h*ot, but with tongue against the roof of the mouth
ṇ—as in *n*ut, but with tongue against the roof of the mouth
t—as in t*u*b, but with tongue against the teeth
th—as in ligh*t-h*eart, but with tongue against the teeth
p—as in *p*ine
ph—as in u*ph*ill (not pronounced like *f*)
b—as in *b*ird
bh—as in ru*b-h*ard
m—as in *m*other
y—as in *y*es
r—as in *r*un
l—as in *l*ight
v—as in *v*ine
ś (palatal)—as in the *s* in the German word *s*prechen
ṣ (cerebral)—as the *sh* in *sh*ine
s (dental)—as in *s*un
h—as in *h*ome

Special Letters

ṁ (anusvāra)—a resonant nasal like the *n* in the French word *bon*
ḥ (visarga)—a final, echoed h-sound: *aḥ* is pronounce like *aha*; *iḥ* like *ihi*.

Glossary

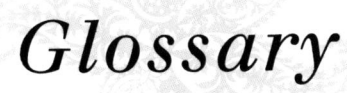

ĀCAMANA
: purification ritual performed before worship requiring a little Ganges water and the chanting of some mantras.

ARTHA
: economic development; one of the four main goals of human life.

ĀSANA
: a sitting place, usually for performing yoga.

ĀTMĀ-TATTVA
: all that pertains to the real nature of the soul.

AVATĀRA
: one who descends from the spiritual platform for the benefit of the conditioned souls.

BHAKTI
: devotion to the Supreme Lord

BHAKTI-YOGA
: the practice of the path of devotion to the Supreme Lord

BHĀVA
: intense feeling of devotional ecstasy

BRAHMĀ
: the creator appointed by the Supreme Lord to manifest the material universe and supervise its development.

BRAHMACĀRĪ
: a celibate student of spiritual science

BRAHMAN
: spirit; the omnipresent life force; also called Param Brahman, the Supreme Spirit.

BRĀHMAṆA
: one of the four occupational classes of human society, comprised of teachers, priests and advisors.

BRAHMĀNANDA

the happiness experienced by realizing Brahman, the real nature and identity of all life.

CIT-ŚAKTI

the potency of knowledge; one of the three spiritual potencies of the Supreme Lord (the other two being sat and ānanda, eternity and happiness).

DARŚANA

a personal meeting with a great saint or the Lord Himself.

DEVA

a demigod; an inhabitant of the heavenly planets; the devas are in charge of managing the material universe.

DHARMA

duty or religious duty according to one's qualities and position; one of the four main goals of human life.

GṚHASTHA

a married or family man, who "lives at home".

GUṆA

quality; the three main material qualities are goodness (sattva), passion (rajas) and ignorance (tamas).

GURU

a teacher or master; usually spiritual master.

JĪVĀ

the individual infinitesimal soul.

JÑĀNA

knowledge, pursuance of knowledge.

KALPA

a day of Brahmā, composed of 1000 cycles of four ages, for a total of several hundred thousand years of our planet; at the end of this period, the universe is subject to a partial destruction.

KĀMA

material enjoyment; one of the four goals of human life.

KARMA
action; pursuance of action; results of action.

KṚṢṆA-KATHĀ
all talks that refer to Śrī Krishna, His devotees, His devotion, etc.

KṢATRIYA
one of the four occupational groups of human society; it includes warriors, administrators, rulers, managers, etc.

LĪLĀ
play; pastime; divine adventure.

LOTUS FEET
the Lord and His devotees are described as having lotus feet because they are never contaminated by matter although descending to this world, just as the lotus flower is always clean, pure and fragrant although it lives and sprouts from muddy waters.

MAHAT-TATTVA
the total sum of the material energy, from which all the material elements arise.

MANTRA
a special sound, word or sentence charged with spiritual powers.

MĀYĀ
magic or illusion; something that is not what it seems to be.

MOKṢA
liberation; one of the four goals of human life.

MUNI
a silent sage who engages in meditation and introspection, often dedicating all his time to study.

NĀRĀYAṆA-ASTRA
the weapon of Nārāyaṇa, charged with the spiritual potency of the Supreme Lord.

PARIKRAMA
a holy pilgrimage to sacred places where the Lord or His devotees have performed spiritual activities.

PRĀṆA
life force; transported by air and breath, it moves the body and makes it work.

PRĀṆAYAMA
control over the life force through breathing exercises.

PREMA-BHAKTI
love and devotion; usually refers to the feelings of ecstasy in devotion to the Supreme Lord.

PŪJĀ
rituals of worship.

PURŪṢA
enjoyer; person; male; sometimes refers to the Supreme Lord in relation to the living entities who are His prakṛti, and sometimes refers to the conditioned living entity who wants to dominate and enjoy the material nature (prakṛti).

ṚṢI
A sage or saintly person.

SĀDHANA
regular spiritual practice of purification, meditation, study and worship according to a specific schedule.

SĀDHU
saint; good person; renounced person who is fully dedicated to spiritual life.

SAMĀDHI
the state of undisturbed meditation wherein the intelligence is steady, enabling one to see things clearly as actually they are; the final stage of yoga wherein one's spiritual nature is fully realized.

SAṀSĀRA
cycle of birth and death; conditioned life.

SANNYĀSĪ
renounced saint who has no material possessions, prestige or duties and who dedicates himself fully to spiritual life.

SATTVA-GUṆA
goodness; one of the three main material qualities.

ŚĀSTRA
revealed scripture that has been transmitted traditionally in a disciplic succession.

SIDDHA
perfect being; either living on this planet (especially yogis) or on higher planets.

SUPREME LORD
The Supreme Personality of Godhead has many names, such as Krishna, Vishnu, Nārāyaṇa, Hari, Govinda, Acyuta, Bhuta Bhavana, etc. All these names refer to the same Supreme Person and indicate His many qualities and activities.

TAPASYA
austerity performed according to the scriptures; it usually consists of refraining from sense enjoyment and voluntary penance.

VAIṢṆAVA
devotee of Vishnu or Krishna.

VĀNAPRASTHA
one of the four stages of human life; a retired period prior to sannyas, when the practitioner leaves home and goes to some holy place (or forest hermitage) to develop detachment from family life and material enjoyment.

VINA
musical instrument used by the great saint and sage Nārada Muni.

YAJÑA
Vedic sacrifice involving offerings to the Lord and His representatives, chanting of hymns, distribution of sanctified food and other gifts, etc.

YOGA
practice to develop control over one's lower self.

YOGI
one who practices yoga.

notes

notes

notes